TWELVE WATCH BUYER'S JOURNAL – TO INSPIRE AND EMPOWER WATCH LOVERS WITH INFORMED AND TOPICAL KNOWLEDGE.

This publication is not a guide, but can be a factual reference. It is not a 'map' of the watch industry, but a highlighted route through the depth of knowledge available. It is intended to entertain you, as much as inform.

This journal will help you strengthen your passion and relationship with watches, and enlighten you beyond what you already know.

The average watch buyer is one of the most discerning and resourceful consumers in the world, and we aim to support and hone their behaviour, and promote watch buying as not only a wonderful hobby, but a valuable skill.

Work And Play Ltd
8a Lonsdale Road,
London,
NW6 6RD

Published by Work And Play Limited
www.weareworkandplay.com

Copyright © Work and Play Ltd 2014

All rights reserved. No content in this publication may be reproduced or distributed, by any means or in any form, electronically or mechanically (including photocopying, recording, photographing or use of any other storage or retrieval system) without prior written permission from the copyright holder and above publisher of this book.

ISBN 978 0 9928376 0 0

Art Direction: Dan Rolfe Johnson

Images credited on page, from multiple and various sources

Printed on behalf of Latitude Press Limited

CONTENTS

INTRODUCTION..
1 UNDERSTANDING VALUE....................................
2 BUYING VS COLLECTING...................................
3 COMPLICATIONS..
4 LONGEVITY..
5 MATERIALS SCIENCE......................................
6 CASE MANUFACTURING ....
7 HOW TO COLLECT ....
8 THE INTERNET ....
9 AUCTION INDEX ....
10 BRANDS AND MILESTONES ....
11 OBSERVATORY COMPETITIONS ....
12 INDUSTRY PROFILES ....

EDITORIAL BOARD

Simon de Burton

Simon de Burton writes about high-end watches for publications around the world, including the Financial Times, the Daily Telegraph, Vanity Fair and GQ. He acquired his first mechanical watch at the age of six (a white-dialled Westclox) but only discovered the true wonders of haute horlogerie while working at auction house Sotheby's during the early 1990s, where he was infected by the enthusiasm of legendary colleagues such as Dr George Daniels, Tina Millar and Daryn Schnipper.

Ken Kessler

Ken Kessler has been deeply involved with watches for 35 years, first as a collector, then as a dealer in vintage pieces. He has written about watches for Wall Street Journal, Financial Times, The Telegraph, QP, GQ, Men's Health, Top Gear, Esquire and over 100 other titles. Also an authority on high-end audio, Ken has produced four hi-fi histories. His weaknesses include chronographs, military and diving watches, music, crime fiction and Italian wine.

Andrew Hildreth

Dr. Andrew Hildreth is respected throughout the watch industry as a leading authority on high-end timepieces. Dr. Hildreth is a co-founding editorial board member of Twelve Watch Buyers Journal and sits on the editorial advisory panel. He is also a senior member and moderator on PuristSPro.com, the website and forum used by dedicated watch collectors and connoisseurs, and has written widely (both on PuristSPro and other publications such as QP and iW) on leading brands such as Richard Mille, Jaeger-LeCoultre, and Greubel Forsey. Dr. Hildreth is a Jury Member on the "00/24 Watch of the Year" awards. He is a Freeman of the City of London through the Worshipful Company of Clockmakers, and also a Fellow of the Royal Statistical Society. Dr. Hildreth gained his Ph.D from the University of Cambridge, and is a former Professor of Economics at the University of California, Berkeley, he now lives and works in London as a Partner/Managing Director at consultancy Alvarez & Marsal LLP.

Jacob Tomkins

Jacob is the founder, chief editor and publisher of Twelve. He is a watch enthusiast with a professional background in luxury brand strategy and consultancy, and niche journal publishing. He has worked privately for watch buyers for several years sourcing rare and investible watches, and has gathered valuable and substantial collecting knowledge while growing his fascination with the mechanics and variations in horology. This journal represents his vision to bring knowledge of watch making and collecting to life through intellectual analysis and study, and also a passion for beautiful print design and information architecture. Jacob works as a design and strategic brand development consultant.

INTRODUCTION

WELCOME TO TWELVE

One is confronted with many questions when deciding which watch to buy. The answers to these questions are different for every person and in every situation. Watches are status symbols, works of art, innovations, sports accessories, fashion items, dare I even say investments. Some are all of the above.

Why watches are fascinating and captivating objects is an easier question to answer; for me anyway.

Watches are a magnificent achievement of human science and creative ability. The best mechanical pieces are some of the most complex hand made machines available to the every day consumer. One can pick up a luxury mechanical timepiece in nearly any shopping promenade or mall in the world. These tiny mechanical devices measure time and track the planets almost perfectly. They are entirely powered by dozens or even hundreds of especially crafted materials and parts, all operating in mechanical unison - hand assembled in most cases - and without the need for maintenance or repair, in some, for decades.

Strangely, horology as a time keeping technology is obsolete. New timing devices have become accurate to the standards of electromagnetic frequency and measurements of atomic decay in the case of the atomic clocks we have today. These industrial devices transmit exact time around the world to digital clocks and watches automatically, with total precision. Regardless of horological instruments' relative recent technological obsolescence, they are still central to a thriving and inspirational luxury brand industry. We have these manufacturers and visionary brands to thank for being surrounded by so many impressive and ever evolving products. The tremendous beauty, craftsmanship and mechanics which go into these products make the industry as a whole uniquely interesting.

My fascination started as a child, first witnessing the magical, unending, consistent swinging of a great-uncle's grandfather clock pendulum. Not knowing of the key that wound it, it appeared to tick and tock forever on its own, needing no assistance to guide us through our day. As a small child this connection with how the day was laid out was where fantasy met reality. Even learning of horology later in life, the magic never died for me. This early childhood fascination has not faded, still driving my interest in the scientific precision needed to achieve the best horological design.

Having spent years trying to sharpen my focus, I naturally absorbed a breadth of knowledge. This has served me well in working closely with buyers to create meaningful collections, which also increase in value over time. It is only through a long term accumulation of information that I could start to form my own ideas of how real value could be found in mechanical watches, but I knew that with enough knowledge, the right buying decision for my clients could be made. As Albert Einstein said; "Information is not knowledge".

Twelve does not set out to be a guide to train the reader to be an expert buyer. It aims to be a thought provoking document sharing worlds of fascination and topical subjects to strengthen an admirer's knowledge. It presents the facts and information which might turn a mere buyer into an enthusiast, or an 'accumulator' into a collector (as Simon de Burton writes in chapter 2). We want to inspire the enthusiast, as well as influence the novice. While this may be a challenge to accomplish, we have set out to do so by combining hard facts and data with anecdotal insight and focused perspective, all presented by well-known writers with deep experience and self-interest.

Twelve's intention is to aggregate and analyse those areas of knowledge which have attracted my fellow writers and me to watches as enthusiasts and led us to become experienced collectors. We hope the content will provide a platform for readers to develop their own insights and continue to build further knowledge.

Twelve's aim is to provide new insights from key opinion leaders and anecdotal articles from the industry's best writers. All content is unique, original and intended to entertain as much as educate. You will not find our articles on blogs or in any magazine; the content is bespoke for our hard copy readers.

WATCHES AS INVESTMENTS

Investing in watches was in a bygone age considered a crude concept, but is now a fascinating topic. Much like collecting art, not every collector can be a successful investor. We hope to show that watches can often be solid investments, dispelling the myth that collections cannot increase in value. It is becoming considered shrewd to invest in easily tradable, high value watches. There are even funds open to the public for investment into watch portfolios. These concepts are still in their infancy compared to other investment sectors. The fact that watches can be traded, sold or worn gives them an special attraction, not just to wise investors, but to trend-followers and trend-setters. We ask our interviewees in Chapter 12 – 'Industry Profiles' their opinions on this topic.

Twelve is about information. A fascination with watches but lack of funds led me to gather information in my early career, rather than timepieces themselves. This knowledge has been my treasured reward. The journal shares this information, but like a watch it is also designed as an elegant reference piece, which complements the products themselves - as much a pleasure to hold, as it is a wealth of insight.

WHY THE NUMBER TWELVE?

Clearly there is one parallel between the number 12 and clocks and watches. But more than this, we can venture into the history books to find 12 comes up in many significant forms throughout world history and science. For example, there are twelve 'Jacobian elliptic functions' – the mathematical principles behind the swinging of a pendulum, twelve months to the year, twelve signs of the Zodiac, twelve tribes of Israel, twelve days of Christmas, twelve human cranial nerves; the list goes on. It is regarded as a magical number, which fits the magic we find in horology. A memorable, trustworthy number, as reliable as anything can be.

The history of the number twelve and its relationship to time keeping or counting dates back to pre-literate times, perhaps 'cave-men times': Each hand has twelve knuckles – three to each finger minus the thumb – which allowed people to count to twelve on one hand using the thumb. This is said to be the earliest origins of the number's multiple uses in society, which then led to the day's split into twelve sections. This, of course, far predates horology and time keeping as we know it today.

There will be twelve annual issues that make up the complete series of the Twelve Journal, each with twelve chapters. Each chapter will address a stand-alone subject of interest to readers.

TWELVE CHAPTERS

The content is split amongst several writers with varied expertise and talent. Throughout the progress of the publication, we will build the case for understanding value and explain technical aspects of watch making and particularly interesting models in clear language. This first issue is intended to be a broad look at the entire market and watchmaking as a whole. There will be a short editorial introduction to most chapters

THE AUTHORS AND THEIR SUBJECTS

Simon De Burton explains the mystery behind various complications. Jonathan Scatchard helps us to ensure our timepieces last as long as they should through care and maintenance. We, along with Stephen J. Pulvirent and Robert-Jan Broer, cover the importance of the internet in the buyers' life and analyse how it has affected the watch market. Ken Kessler gives us a chapter dedicated to being a structured collector. We also go into some detail on manufacturing capabilities and materials, aiming to enlighten and furnish even the more experienced watch aficionado with new facts and tantalising realities.

One of our most important and unique chapters is our novel Auction Index. Compiled by Andrew Hildreth, it is aimed at giving readers a view of which brands and movements command increasing auction prices. The index is compiled from data by scanning recent history to track the performance of particular pieces over time. There will be one excerpt from our index published in each issue of the journal, plus ongoing analysis and publication of similarly important data and information on the Twelve website throughout the year.

Later issues in the series will focus on specific interest areas of horology and watches. There will be dedicated diving watch and chronograph issues as well as military, vintage and high complication as serious areas of collectability.

We hope you enjoy reading as much as we have enjoyed compiling.

Numeral a re-drawing from original artist sketches of a typeface developed specifically for IWC Da Vinci line.

WRISTWATCHES; UNDERSTANDING VALUE
PUBLISHERS INTRODUCTION

Buying something valuable usually means it is expensive. We all know, if we want to buy a 'valuable' watch, we may be considering spending thousands. A question many non-watch lovers ask is "why does a watch cost so much?!"

There are relatively few other luxury products available capable of retaining their value and therefore considered a potential investment. Compared to handbags or jewellery for example – both are generally depreciating products, costing as much and more than watches. a perceived value or emotional impact of the product on it's owner. or you could say 'love affair' with the object, is a frequently shared principle of all corners of the luxury industry, and brands achieve higher emotional values by making their retail experiences and marketing campaigns rich, confident and definitive. Other products, however, rarely require the complexity and technical beauty of watches.

Successful brands compel their customers to feel comfortable and associated with their products. This is valuable. Audemars Piguet, as an example, has one of my favourite emotive advertising slogans: "To break the rules, you must first master them". They rightly give the impression they are a well engineered and customer aware brand, with exceptional quality products, both in design and horology. These qualities are shared by many of the top manufacturers, but not always communicated effectively.

Value, however, is really all about the resale price – can you eventually sell the item for more than you bought it? If the answer to this question is yes, then there is investment value in your purchase, and it is collectible.

Most serious collectors will often tell you that they would never sell their watches anyway, so the resale price is not important to them, but you would rarely find an experienced collector buying a piece which is not 'collectible'.

It is no coincidence that in most collectors' collections, the top five brands are strongly represented. I believe these are Patek Philippe, Rolex, Audemars Piguet, Jaeger leCoultre and Cartier, closely followed by Vacheron Constantin, Breguet, A. Lange & Sohne, IWC, Omega, Panerai, Franck Muller and Ulysse Nardin as key historical and highly popular brands in their own right.

These 'top five' are not to be confused with the 'Holy Trinity' which are widely considered to be the pinnacle of watchmaking dynasties, all with around 200 years of horological heritage. These are Patek Philippe, Vacheron Constantin and Breguet – again, closely followed by Audemars Piguet, Jaeger leCoultre and A.Lange Sohne in terms of achievements, heritage and horological respect. These 'Holy Trinity' brands have the most tried and tested designs. They have shaped the luxury watchmaking market over the last 200 years; having the best horologists and the oldest customer lists. These brands also have a huge market saturation due to large collections being available for decades longer than competitors': these are the brands that command the resale market, and often the collectors' hearts.

This is not to say that collectors only buy collectible pieces or brands. Quite the contrary: most collectors will also tell you that they would not buy a watch they do not love – and no two Patek Philippe collectors have exactly the same style. Often advanced collectors will venture away from their staple brand to find something they love elsewhere. The brand will always influence the buying decision, but a collector buying a more unusual, non-mainstream brand is satisfying their emotive desire, more than treating it as a pure investment.

Here Simon de Burton gives us his take on value, and points out three watches which have historically consistently increased in price.

WRIST WATCHES
UNDERSTANDING VALUE

Simon de Burton

Anyone who is seriously enthusiastic about contemporary luxury watches will be well aware that the brands charge a hefty premium for allowing us the privilege of strapping their wares to our wrists. It is only necessary to observe the level of spend on marketing to see only a fraction of the 'RRP' of a watch is accounted for by the required craftsmanship and materials.

Indeed, it is fairly well known there is usually a price hike of at least fifty per cent between factory gates and retail store - a figure that, in some cases, can even rise to as much as eighty per cent.

As in the world of new cars, the majority of new watches plummet in value the moment they are sold.. Some, however, hold their value surprisingly well, while some even prove to be sound investments. But how does a buyer sort the wheat from the chaff?

The answer is to know what defines 'value' in a watch. What makes one chronograph in a jeweller's window more valuable than another? What makes one pre-owned dive watch twice as valuable as a similar looking one, with a similar mechanism, but a different name on the dial?

Broadly speaking, the answer is exactly that: the name on the dial. It is only necessary to look at a catalogue from one of the high-end specialist watch houses to see that there areonly a handful of blue-chip names consistently proven to perform exceptionally on the residual market.

At the top of the tree - by a long way - is Patek Philippe. Most of the collectable pieces made between the 1940s and the 1980s frequently sell for sums in excess of $2m which sets it well ahead of Rolex, its nearest rival,. Rolex has only recently seen one of its vintage models breach the $1 million mark. Indeed, Patek has made marketing hay from the heirloom status of its products with the advertising slogan "You never actually own a Patek Philippe - you merely look after it for the next generation."

Patek Philippe Perpetual Calendar Chronograph

Rolex Submariner Comex
Photo: Watch Club

Nevertheless, it is Rolex that offers some of the best value products in contemporary watch making - if not some of the best value products across the board - because models such as the Submariner, GMT Master and Cosmograph are invariably worth more than they cost new even after a decade or more of use.

The reason for this is quite simple: they are well made, reliable watches with broad appeal and come from one of the best known brands. By doing what it does best and not straying in to the high-cost world of complicated tourbillons, minute repeaters, perpetual calendars and so on, Rolex has established a world-wide reputation as a maker of some of the best quality, best value, no-nonsense watches on the market.

But where do you find value of you do not want a Rolex or a Patek Philippe? Now, you must look for those famous watch marketing words 'history' and 'authenticity'. Quite simply, this means seeking out a long-standing, high-end brand not prone to producing gimmicks, suddenly changing direction or hastily expanding its range.

A brand of true value could be one which is quietly confident about its design philosophy, only expanding its offerings rarely. A good example of a maker which expanded its repertoire rapidly is Zenith, the historic dial name which became famous for its high-beat El Primero chronograph movement. During the 'noughties,' the then-management sought to bring it to the fore by producing unusual-looking pieces which seemed to stray from the true ethos of the brand as a maker of high quality, classic-looking watches, hurting its balance sheet.

Since Jean-Frederic Dufour took over the helm in 2009, however, Zenith has majored on modern interpretations of historic pieces and played heavily on its past - a strategy which has proved hugely successful.

Names that can never be accused of losing their way, however, include Omega, Vacheron Constantin, Jaeger-LeCoultre, IWC, Audemars Piguet and Girard-Perregaux, all of which have a rich history to go with long-proven watch making skills. The value of their products is therefore intrinsic.

But it is also possible to have 'value' without having history. Take, for example, the work of modern masters such as F.P. Journe, Richard Mille, Greubel Forsey and MB&F. All are relative beginners compared with centuries old brands such as Vacheron and Patek - but by a difficult to achieve combination of intelligent innovation, superb workmanship, respect for their craft and individualism, they have succeeded in attracting a whole new breed of watch enthusiast.

And, if it seems as though it might not be possible to find a young brand making relatively conventional watches which do not cost the earth yet stand out from the rest, think again. One example that springs to mind is Bremont, the pilot watch maker that has gone from a standing start in 2007 to making 6,000 watches per year.

Against all the odds, it has entered one of the most competitive sectors of the watch business and, despite having no history to build on, succeeded in attracting buyers from around the world with its authenticity, imaginative (but not outlandish) products, fair pricing and, above all, the promise of something different.
Ingredients which have, it seems, given its watches the sort of 'value' that many more pretentious brands would like to be credited with.

R.W. Smith Open Dial
Photo: R.W. Smith

THREE WATCHES WITH ADDED VALUE

1

ROLEX SUBMARINER

Introduced at the Basel watch show in 1954, the Submariner remains instantly recognisable 60 years later. It is the dive watch by which all others are judged and still succeeds, as a period advertising campaign proclaimed, in 'looking as good with a dinner suit as with a wet suit.' Gradually and carefully developed over the decades, Submariners are reliable and robust daily wearers which, if properly cared for, are as good as money in the bank.

2
PATEK PHILIPPE PERPETUAL CALENDAR CHRONOGRAPHS

No Patek Philippe wrist watch is cheap, and its high complication pieces are only attainable by the exceedingly well-heeled. But their value is difficult to dispute. The best known references are the 1518 - the first perpetual calendar chronograph to be produced in series - and its successor, the 2499, which remained in production from 1950 until the mid 1980s. The right examples can easily fetch seven figure sums, making the current Reference 5204 perpetual calendar, split seconds chronograph seem something of a bargain at a little more than £200,000.....

3
RW SMITH SERIES 2

The legendary English horologist Dr George Daniels -inventor of the celebrated Co-Axial movement - only ever had one apprentice. His name was Roger Smith, and he has now succeeded Daniels as about the only person in the world to be making watches in the true English tradition, almost entirely by hand. His Series II pieces, currently in production at his Isle of Man workshop, are exquisite examples of the horologists art and the very epitomy of 'value' in a wristwatch. They cost around £90,000 - but your children may thank you for buying one.

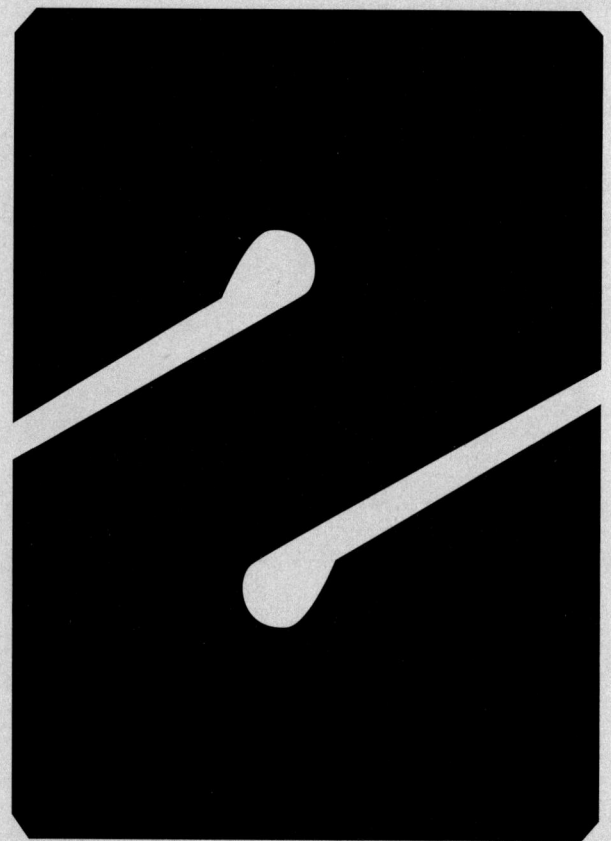

Numeral taken from the dial of an IWC pilots watch

BUYING VERSUS COLLECTING:
PUBLISHERS INTRODUCTION

Simon de Burton now tells us a little about the market and how collecting is fast moving from a dusty, dull exercise based around old pocket watches, to one of the most respected and stable areas of investment for the wealthy.

Buying watches has without a doubt become a serious investment area for wealthy individuals around the world, as Simon has eloquently supported in the previous article. Widely considered to be valuable, transportable assets — one can even invest in watch funds these days. Not all watches are investible however, or even hold their value.

In fact the majority of the global spend on watches goes to purchasing pieces which immediately decrease in value much like cars, and can be thought of as 'luxury' purchases in the everyday sense. Fashion and marketing appear to affect people's buying choices more than the item's intrinsic value.

This is largely because of a lack of accessible knowledge and information, unless you are exceptionally tenacious in your searches. If watch lovers are more informed about the products, they make wiser buying decisions. Things have of course changed dramatically since the growth of the Internet, which we discuss further in Chapter 8. The free availability of online advice and information has seen the birth of new kinds of brands. These brands do not try to dazzle and seduce with diamonds, heritage, fancy logos or design. Instead they use groundbreaking movements, which challenge even the two hundred year old standards of time keeping and hand-made production — or new materials to improve the function and longevity of a watch. Brands are trying to be desirable to informed, knowledgeable buyers, thereby creating a high level of demand for their low production runs, therefore making pieces sought after and valuable.

This is not to say it would be a better world if people bought only objects which would increase in value. In fact quite the opposite. I like the idea of collectors supporting the future potential value of products by purchasing them in their infancy, but here lies a question; how do the big brands ensure their weaker, less impressive products survive if a more discerning and knowledgeable market place develops? Buying watches for the sake of buying might become a thing of the past, but the difference in the behaviour of a 'buyer' and a 'collector is; how much is the customer prepared and able to research the subject?

Do people who buy non-investible watches and luxury products without potential return do so because they have too much money? Do they not care about buying an item with lower value than its price-tag? Quite the opposite. Some people will spend tens of thousands of pounds on a suit or dress, which will last a year or two at most, so even if a watch retains fifty per cent of its value over a decade, but the buyer loves it, it could be considered a better purchase than most fashion items. No two buyers or buying opportunities are the same.

BUYING
VERSUS
COLLECTING

Simon de Burton

Not so long ago I was speaking to an American tycoon called Bruce Weiner who made a large fortune in the confectionary business and was therefore able to indulge his passion for collecting to a degree that most people can only dream of.

We were talking about his remarkable hoard of micro cars - often referred to coloquially as 'bubble cars' - which extended to more than 200 examples together with 50,000 pieces of microcar literature and a vast quantity of microcar models. He had decided to sell the lot, auctioned it off and walked away a further $5 million richer for his trouble.

What was especially interesting about Weiner, however, is that he was not merely a wealthy man who wanted something to spend his money on, chose microcars and then went out and scooped up the most he could find. No, in his own words, he was a '"collector, not an accumulator". The difference he defined thus: "An accumulator just buys stuff without knowing anything about it. A collector is educated and understands everything there is to know about his subject."

In fact, Weiner admitted to being almost fanatical about the amount of research he puts into everything he collects, from microcars to neon signs, disguised weapons, antique radios, sweets (yes, sweets) and - needless to say - wristwatches.

Now, the very fact that you are reading this book reveals a great deal about the current state of the watch market. As little as 15 years ago, books about wristwatches were dry affairs, produced in tiny numbers and bought by the type of people who others might have unkindly referred to as 'watch geeks' but who were, simply, passionate collectors.

In fact, wristwatches did not really justify recognition as a widespread collecting category until some time in the early 1990s, prior to which 'watch collecting' referred principally to what were known as 'antique' pocket watches.

The auction house Antiquorum can be credited with kick-starting the knowledge base which promoted the wristwatch to being 'officially collectable' during the 1980s by breaking new ground with its scholarly watch catalogues. They outlined the histories of brands and the significance of individual models. The house also

A. Lange & Soehne Pilots Military Watch Collection circa 1940
Photo: Bonhams

introduced a revolutionary grading scale to give an accurate indication of the condition of specific lots.

Antiquorum currently makes available more than 30 years' worth of auction results through its on-line catalogue database, a service which is now used as a valuation guide by collectors and dealers the world over – a similar approach to the auction index created by Twelve to track auction performance of collectible watches, which is collated with all the public and private auction information available rather, than just Antiquorums own data. (Chapter 9).

Along the way, rival houses including Bonhams, Christie's and Sotheby's have seen their watch departments grow from small, rather apologetic affairs which once held entire auctions that barely grossed the commission achieved from the sale of a single, mediocre Impressionist painting, to being serious contributors to the global turnover of their respective organisations. Christie's for example, now routinely shifts more than $20 million worth of lots at its major, twice-yearly watch sales in Geneva.

Along with the burgeoning quantity of dedicated internet sites and the explosion in the quantity of watch-related publications (ranging from specialist magazines to the regular supplements included in national newspapers), the auction houses have been the main cause of the stratospheric rise in the popularity of buying 'pre-owned' wristwatches. A fact that has, of course, dramatically increased the number of people who can be regarded as 'collectors'.

But the definition of the term 'watch collector' is far broader than it used to be. No longer does it just refer, for example, to a scholar of 16th century English verge watches, a dedicated buyer of Rolex 'bubblebacks' or a hoarder of military timepieces made before 1945. Now, a 'collector' is simply someone who likes buying and owning watches of any age, type, make or design and has, let's say, more than two. In other words, Weiner's 'accumulators' now have to be accepted as collectors, too.

At the less scholarly end of the spectrum, therefore, we have the compulsive buyers of brand new - or, alternatively, second-hand but barely worn - contemporary watches who simply cannot resist owning the latest thing.

Perhaps the best examples of such collectors are to be found in Hong Kong and mainland China, from where the market in wrist watch sales has been driven for the past few years.
When he moved to Hong Kong from America in 2011, Charles Tearle, the head of Sotheby's watch division in the Far East, was startled by the difference in the Asian attitude to collecting compared with that of people in the West.

"Most Asian collectors will inevitably have a fairly large number of watches, usually in excess of 50. Also, pieces offered for sale are always in absolutely fabulous condition. The fact is, Asian buyers are simply not interested in any watch which shows signs of wear, damage or restoration. They have to be absolutely immaculate, and preferably complete with boxes, paperwork and any other related material," says Tearle.

"The other interesting difference I have noticed between Asian buyers and western ones is the amount that they wear their watches. If a person buys a watch in the U.S, either new or at auction, I would say that they will generally wear it on a very

Longines Lindbergh Aviators Watch circa 1940
Photo: Bonhams

Left: F.P. Journe Sonnerie Souviraine. Photo: F.P. Journe
Right: A. Lange & Soehne Richard Lange Tourbillon
Pour Le Merite. Photo: A. Lange & Soehne

regular basis for one or two years. In Asia, however, most of the contemporary watches which come in for sale have probably been worn once, twice at the most," he adds.

Currently, therefore, it seems that Asians favour new watches and the most committed are gaining their knowledge of complications and an understanding of rarity by buying recent pieces by independent makers such as Richard Mille, Greubel Forsey and F.P Journe, with certain haute horlogerie watches - notably A. Lange and Sohne's 'Pour le Merite' tourbillon and Patek Philippe's 'Sky Moon' tourbillon - currently being among the most highly prized trophies for the collecting cabinet.

But in order to get Asian buyers 'hooked' on watches in the first place, the brands realise the importance of providing them with exactly what they like, even at the non-complicated end of the scale. It is for this reason that we have seen the recent 'return to classic simplicity' with smaller, slimmer watches more suited to lighter-boned Asians.

Away from the new buyers of the Far East, however, there remains a solid core of truly serious, high end collectors - mostly in the West - who seek-out the rarest of rare pieces from the brand that, in vintage watches at least, stands head and shoulders above the rest: Patek Philippe.

With the record for any wrist watch standing in 2013 at Sfr 6.6 million paid for a Patek World Time in 2002 - and with more recent sales including a $3.9 million for a time-only piece and $3.6 million for a reference 2499 perpetual calendar chronograph that belonged to Eric Clapton - there is no other dial name that comes close to this one in terms of collectability and value.

To put this into perspective, the most expensive Rolex (which was sold at Christie's in May 2013) fetched a 'mere' Sfr 1.1 million.

That means that the most covetable Pateks have attracted a whole new breed of collector - super-rich speculators who are suddenly fascinated by wrist watches. Comparable to the people who now invest in high-end classic Ferraris (indeed, they are often the same people) these are collectors who can afford to buy the very best, blue chip pieces.

By their very nature, such watches are in short supply and, once out of circulation, they become all the more sought after, values rise and, if and when they do re-appear on the market, the prices they achieve become increasingly more astounding. As a result, buyers are as likely to be entirely driven by the opportunity to make large profits as they are by a desire to accumulate a superb watch collection.

But not all Patek collectors are so inclined, of course. When it comes to true enthusiasts, one particular individual who springs to mind is a retired airline executive called Ahmed Al-Ghani whom I was seated beside at a lunch some years ago. At the time, he owned around 100 premium quality wristwatches including 34 Pateks, a Daniel Roth tourbillon and various pieces by Vacheron Constantin.

Of all the collectors I have ever met he was, undoubtedly, among the most passionate having held a fascination with watches since he opened the back of his father's Westend timepiece as a small boy.

Mr. Al-Ghani wore most of his watches on a regular basis - including his very valuable Patek minute repeater — but what really revealed his love of the subject was the fact that he kept a number of Pateks in the hermetically-sealed plastic packaging in which they were delivered.

"I don't do it in the hope of increasing their re-sale value, because I would never sell any of my watches," he told me. "I just feel that by delaying the opening I somehow extend the pleasure of ownership. Any collector will tell you that it is the quest to own something and the almost unbearable waiting that gives the greatest pleasure."

True, we all know about that. Even those who cannot afford to buy the type of high-end pieces in Mr. Al-Ghani's collection. But that, surely, is part of the appeal of wrist watch collecting - it can be indulged in by almost anyone, regardless of budget.

Indeed, now that prices for the most collectable pieces have escalated beyond the means of all but the wealthiest, the appeal of vintage pieces from more affordable makers such as Longines, Omega and IWC is starting to be recognised. Currently, however, the golden rule of collecting is to buy only the very best you can afford — generally speaking, badly restored, damaged or non-original watches are entirely out of favour.

But you do not, of course, need to 'go vintage' to be a collector. As evinced by the new Asian enthusiasts, there are plenty of people who enjoy acquiring smaller or larger numbers of new watches regardless of any financial depreciation.

The fact is, 'collections' often come about these days as a result of an attitude to watch buying that is completely different to that of our forefathers. Whereas they might have owned a single, special watch, men - in particular - have come to regard a 'watch wardrobe' as being entirely normal.

As a result, the watch worn for 24 hours a day, seven days a week for 356 day per year is increasingly becoming a thing of the past among collectors and fashionistas. Now it is not unusual to have a watch for work and watch for the evening; a watch for pursuing your hobbies of motor racing, diving or flying; another to take on holiday and perhaps two or three more which you bought, purely and simply, because you fell in love with them.

That's seven watches already. Look out. You've suddenly become a collector……. or are you just an accumulator?

Patek Philippe 5002p
Photo: Gus Oliver

Numeral taken from the dial of a Vacheron Constantin 1972

COMPLICATIONS
PUBLISHERS INTRODUCTION

We can easily understand our emotional attachment when buying a watch we love. But this journal aims to dissect some of the rational factors, namely the intricate, technical details of watches. Twelve looks at value and interest based on watches' function and place in history of horological development.

It is necessary to understand the function of a watch. Spectacular machines have been produced over the centuries, using different innovative horological functions – 'complications'.. A 'complication' in watchmaking does not, as it may imply, refer to a difficulty in running smoothly. Almost the opposite, in fact. It refers to an element of the watch movement that makes it a more 'complicated' device, or, to an enthusiast - a more beautiful and impressive object. For example; a perpetual calendar, a moon phase or a dualtime complication. A watch which is said to have no complications will still tell the time in minutes, seconds and hours, and in many cases the date of the month from 1-31. The 'chronograph' and simple 'date' are not necessarily considered to be complications in today's world of horological achievements.

Devices which know and display 30 or 31 days in a month, or know which day of the week it is, or which month or year, or even tell you the positioning of the stars, quantify leap years, play the time through the chime of a repeater; these are the devices that contain the real complications. With them go several more layers of interlocking parts, linking cogs, wheels and springs. Adding almost any complication to a regular three-hand movement will at least double its production time sometimes adding up to months or years in order to perfect a single piece. Also required are grand mathematical calculations to ensure all parts move in unison and keep time to an efficient and acceptable margin. Watches with multiple complications are the core of the magical, miniature, mechanical masterpieces that fascinate the collector.

In this chapter we aim to explain the terminology of the various kinds of complications you can find in a fine timepiece. Below, Simon de Burton also takes a look at some of the more complicated watches and famous complications of the past, giving us his insight on these magnificent modifications to time keeping. Andrew Hildreth then explains the technology and history behind a Tourbillon – the ultimate complication for time keeping.

LIST OF COMPLICATIONS
AND OUR DEFINITION:

24-hour watch
A watch where the hour hand completes one revolution every 24hrs, instead of 12hrs.

Automatic watch
A self winding watch, generating energy through a hinged kinetic rotor which responds to the wearer's movements.

Chronograph
For measuring time periods using one or two buttons and sub dials

Double chronograph
Or 'rattrapante' for split second timing more than one subject.

Flyback chronograph
A chronograph that can be reset while running.

Date display
Numbered date wheel turning once per 24hrs, 1-31.

Day of week display
Worded day wheel turning once per 24hrs, Monday - Sunday.

Second time zone
Usually a hand or a sub dial showing the time of day in another time zone.

Equation of time
A display of the difference between 'true' solar time and 'mean' solar time. This is known as an astronomical indication which intends to display the separation between the 'true' solar time and the man made 'mean' solar time. Tracking a sundial across the year against an accurate time keeping device would show there are continual hourly differences.

Display of zone solar time
…as opposed to standard time. Display of truelocal solar time

Display of sidereal time
A mean sidereal day is about 23 hours, 56 minutes, 4.0916 seconds (accounted for by an extra day on the calendar each leap year)

Display of time zones
Multiple time zone indiators.

Time of sunset
A continuously changing calculation throughout the year for a single location's sunset.

Time of sunrise
A continuously changing calculation throughout the year for a single location's sunrise.

Easter date calculators
Hour Repeater – or simply 'repeater' uses hammers and chimes to strike the hour, activated by the push of a button.

Quarter repeater
While a 'repeater' is a chime and hammer which strike to indicate the current hour time through use of a button, this will strike the number of hours and number of quarter hours since the last hour, using two tones of chime, activated by the use of a button.

Five-minute repeater
Strikes the number of hours, i.e. strikes three times for 3 o'clock, and then the number of five minute intervals since the last hour, using two tones of chime. Activated by the use of a button.

Minute repeater
Like a 'quarter repeater' with the additional minutes. So with three tones, strikes the number of hours, number of quarter hours, and then number of minutes since the last quarter hour.

Decimel Repeater
As a minute repeater, but after striking the hours, strikes the number of ten minute intervals since the last hour, before striking the single extra minutes.

Grande Sonnerie
Strikes automatically every quarter hour totell the time in hours and quarters, and can also strike the hours at the push of a button.

Dumb repeater
A repeater used to tell the time quietly, where a hammer strikes a block, so the vibrations or 'thud' can be felt by the wearer.

Passing strike
A watch that chimes, perhaps every hour or quarter hour.

Alarm
A fixed set time for the watch to make a sound.

Month display
In words or numbers, indicating the month.

Sign of the Zodiac
Shows in which one of the twelve 30O ecliptic regions the wearer is located.

Display of leap year
Showing year 1-4 of each leap year cycle.

Moon phases
Indicator showing the fullness of the moon.

Mechanised star chart
Moving chart of the stars above a fixed point on earth.

Astrolabe dial
A dial designed to help track the position of the sun, stars and planets.

Perpetual calendar
Display of the correct date, taking into account different lengths of month and leap years.

Annual calendar
Date display, taking into account only the varying month lengths. Requires annual resetting on 1st March.

Power reserve
Indicator of remaining power held in the watch, through the tension of the mainspring.

Quickset date
Date function that is easily set through minimal crown function

Week of year
Number indicating 0-52 weeks in the year.

Dead second
Second hand that divides up each second with more than one fractional movement.

Foudroyante
Second hand on a chronograph that completes an entire rotation of the dial every second, sometimes with fractional divisions breaking up the second.

Tourbillon
(Considered by some to not be a complicationbut rather a mechanical refinement – pleaserefer to "The Tourbillon" article at the end of this chapter).

Time signal processor
Tells the time.

COMPLICATIONS

Simon De Burton

While most of us seek a life less complicated, horologists have habitually sought to make their lives as difficult as possible - as far as their work is concerned, at any rate. No sooner had the first watch been created towards the close of the 15th century (thanks to the invention of the coiled spring which made timekeepers portable) then the people who made them were adding functions above and beyond that of normal timekeeping to introduce what we now commonly call 'complications'.

In one of his sonnets, the Italian poet Gaspar Visconti described "Certain small and portable clocks made with a little ingenuity, and which are continually going, showing the hours, many courses of the planets, the festivals, and striking when the time requires it."

Nowadays, such a timepiece might fairly be described as 'a repeating astronomical calendar alarm watch', which would be impressive enough even in the 21st century. Cynics might say that the fact that Visconti died in 1499 shows, perhaps, just how far we have not come.

It was only during the course of the following three centuries, however, that horologists gradually conceived, developed and refined the complications that first appeared in pocket watches and which, since the first quarter of the 20th century, have been downsized and adapted to the wristwatch format.
In 1687, for example, London watch maker Daniel Quare was granted a patent for his quarter repeating mechanism; the first minute repeaters followed less than 20 years later; Antoine Lepine is credited with devising the first truly 'perpetual' calendar watch in 1770 and the chronograph was patented by Nicolas Rieussec in 1822.

In between came mechanisms to display sidereal time (calculated on the Earth's rate of rotation in relation to stars, rather than the sun) and indicators to show everything from the age and phases of the moon to the times of sunset and sunrise, the hour in different time zones and the 'equation' of time (the difference between the real solar time and that based on exact, 24-hour days).

Add to that moon phase indication, grande sonnerie chimes, elapsed time mechanisms to allow split-seconds recording and the 'foudroyant' function which allows a chronograph hand to make a complete rotation of the dial in various fractions of a minute, and it becomes apparent that the most inventive watch makers have seldom felt constrained by the apparently limited space of the universe in which they work.

But such innovations were not merely the result of makers' desires to test their own abilities. More commonly, they were the solutions to genuine problems that needed to be addressed.

The repeating mechanism, for example, made it possible to easily know the time in the poor lighting conditions which prevailed until the invention of forms of illumination that were more effective than the candle or the oil lamp; the moon phase provided a way of tracking the the movements of the Earth's only natural satellite when its waxing and waning was vital to navigation and agriculture; the chronograph, combined with simple telemetric, tachymetric or pulsometer scales, could be used for anything from measuring a patient's heart rate to predicting the distance of military ordnance.

And it is the latter which, despite having become ubiquitous, can still be considered to be one of the most difficult complications to execute. Although the original mechanism was invented by Louis Moinet in 1816, it was Frenchman Rieussec who advanced the idea forward in developing a contraption for timing horse races which took the form of a wooden box containing revolving discs on which times were recorded with an ink stylus.

This basic mechanism was refined and reduced in size in order to become viable for pocket watch use, but it was not until the first military aircraft appeared during World War One that, in 1915, Gaston Breitling devised a wrist chronograph that was built from scratch (as opposed to being a pocket watch converted for the wrist). The invention proved a boon to wartime pilots who appreciated the convenience of not having to fumble for a pocket watch while wearing their cumbersome flying gear, and by the late 1930s Breitling had been made official supplier to the Royal Air Force.

The chronograph's complexity stems from the fact that it requires a series of train wheels (a chronograph which records elapsed time periods of 12 hours, 60 minutes and 30 seconds will, for example, use three) to be instantly engaged with or disengaged from the main mechanism without affecting the normal timekeeping functions of hours, seconds and minutes.

In addition to using a considerable amount of energy, the chronograph function can also prove delicate and its mechanism must be carefully synchronised to prevent seizure. The simplest and least expensive chronographs have 'lever' movements in which levers, activated directly from the push pieces, cause the relevant gears to mesh with the main drive train in order to start and stop the train wheels.

The more sophisticated column wheel incorporates a cylinder which begins to rotate when the pushpiece is activated. Levers fall between castellations at the top of the cylinder to drive the chronograph functions, although the majority of modern chronographs are cam actuated and rely on the buttons acting on a heart-shaped cam which serves to start, stop and reset the train wheels.

Beyond basic calendar functions, the chronograph is undoubtedly the complication most often seen on modern wristwatches. But perhaps even more practical is the ability to show the time in more than one of the world's locations.

In its simplest form, this can be had in 'GMT' watches which feature either a secondary hour hand or a digital hour disc in order to display both home time and local time. A true 'world time' watch, however, is capable of displaying the time in 24 or more locations simultaneously.

It was a genius watch maker called Louis Cottier who created the first world time pocket watch in 1931, a masterpiece of micro mechanics that was so fiendishly clever that it simultaneously showed the time in more than a dozen of the most important cities by means of a marked, rotating disc that was synchronised with the main home time indication.

Within a year, Vacheron Constantin had collaborated with Cottier to produce its first World Time watch, the Reference 3372, which made it possible to instantly read-off the time in 31 cities around the world. Other makers, including Patek Philippe, adopted the system and, in 2011, Vacheron developed it into a watch which is capable of displaying the hour in all 37 current time zones.

For horological connoisseurs, however, there is one complication that stands head and shoulders above the others - and that is the 'grand sonnerie' which contrives to marry a quarter striking mechanism with a repeater. On the quarter-hour, it strikes the number of hours on its first gong, followed by the number of quarter-hours since the top of the hour on a second gong.

A grand sonnerie watch can also strike the hours on demand, usually by means of a slide which, when pushed, recharges the spring which drives the mechanism.

FOUR OF THE MOST COMPLICATED WATCHES EVER MADE:

1

THE HENRY GRAVES SUPERCOMPLICATION POCKET WATCH

The Patek Philippe Graves Supercomplication was completed in 1933 at the behest of New York banking tycoon Henry Graves Jnr. It contains 900 parts, has two dials, nine sub dials and eighteen hands. In addition to the usual timekeeping functions, it displays the times of sunrise and sunset and has a full perpetual calendar which compensates for the omission of a Leap Year every fourth century. In total, the watch boasts 24 functions — including Grand Sonnerie chimes -- and incorporates an accurate star chart showing the night sky as seen from New York. The watch remained the most complicated in the world until 1989, when Patek surpassed it with the 33-complication Calibre 89 made to mark its 150th anniversary. The Graves Supercomplication remains, however, the greater horological legend - not least because it changed hands for £6.8 million at auction in December 1999, making it the most valuable watch in the world.

2
VACHERON CONSTANTIN
TOUR DE L'ILE

In 2005, Vacheron Constantin created the Tour de L'Ile to mark its 250th anniversary. With sixteen complications, it bested Patek Phiippe's Sky Moon Tourbillon by four functions to become, at the time, 'the most complicated wristwatch ever made'. Like the Patek, it features sidereal time, a perpetual calendar, date, days of the week, months, the four-year cycle, ages and phases of the moon and a minute repeater. The Vacheron exceeds all this with the inclusion of a second time zone, equation of time, grande sonnerie and power reserve. It should be noted that, in both watches, the inclusion of a tourbillon regulator was
marked down as a 'complication' although, as is explained elsewhere in this journal, it is not, officially, considered to be so as it does not add an extra feature beyond the usual function of timekeeping. The Tour de L'Ile wristwatch sold at auction for Sfr1,876,250 in April 2005.

3

JAEGER-LECOULTRE
DUOMETRE
GRANDE SONNERIE

Unveiled in 2009 as part of Jaeger-Le Coultre's highly exclusive set of haute horlogerie watches called 'Hybris Meccanica,' the Duometre Grande Sonnerie claimed a world record, for a wristwatch, of 26 separate functions, the most impressive being a mechanism that plays Big Ben's celebrated Westminster Chimes from beginning to end on special, square-section gongs that are attached to the crystal and can be altered in tone to suit the requirements of the buyer. The Duometre Grande Sonnerie has 17 patents and contains a remarkable 1,300 components in a mechanism that incorporates other classic haute horlogeric touches such as a flying tourbillon, retrograde displays and a perpetual calendar programmed until the year 2100. On launch, it could only be bought as part of a Euros 1.8 million set of three, along with the Gyrotourbillon and the Reverso a Triptyque.

4

FRANCK MULLER
AETERNITAS MEGA 4

Since 2010, Franck Mueller's Aeternitas Mega 4 has held the title of 'world's most complicated wristwatch' thanks to its remarkable 36 complications delivered through 1,483 components. In addition to the 'usual' functions found on such pieces, it boasts a few extras such as automatic winding for both the main movement and its Westminster carillon, two additional time zones, a monopusher, split seconds chronograph and a perpetual calendar programmed for 1,000 years. The majority of the complications - 25 - are visible from the dial side, which presents its plethora of information in a surprisingly legible format. Again, the tourbillon is included among the list of functions, but even discounting it still leaves the Mega 4 way ahead of its rivals in terms of complexity. The watch allegedly took five years to develop and is, understandably, being made in extremely limited numbers. The price is currently believed to be somewhere around the $3 million mark.....

THE
TOURBILLON

Andrew Hildrith

A little over two hundred years ago, Abraham-Louis Breguet filed his patent for the tourbillon stating that he had: "… succeeded in cancelling … the anomalies caused by the different positions of the centers of gravity … allow the oiling of the friction surfaces to always be even … and finally to cancel many other causes of error influencing movement accuracy." It was, and is, a remarkable achievement for any watchmaker. Breguet had been concerned with forces acting on the lever escapement that would regulate the time keeping properties of the watch. Variations had been noticed in the accuracy of the watch depending on whether or not it was lying flat on the desk (horizontal), or hanging on the watch stand or sitting in the waistcoat pocket (vertical). After all, the tourbillon was originally developed for the pocket watch. Part of the problem (as the quote suggests) was due to gravity; part of the problem was due to the viscosity of lubricating oils in the eighteenth century.

Having been spirited out of Paris by his friend David Marat, and on the run from the Revolutionary Council, Breguet went to Geneva and then to London. In London, he met John Arnold and the two become firm friends. Their two sons were apprenticed to the other as a sign of both mutual respect and friendship

Depending on what you ask or read concerning the definition of 'forces acting on the escapement', the tourbillon was either a mechanism to counter the effects of gravity; or to counter the effects of poor lubrication distribution over the surfaces that held and allowed the balance wheel to rotate freely. While the more widely accepted view of the purpose for the tourbillon: to counteract the effects of gravity, is given by most in the industry (for example, by Robert Greubel and Stephen Forsey) the more minority view is held by F.P. Journe. With modern oils being far more efficient and stable, the need to evenly maintain oil on the friction surfaces has declined as a reason for the tourbillon escapement. Hence, modern proponents of the tourbillon concentrate on the gravity defying aspects and the ability to maintain the timing of the balance wheel.

Irrespective of exactly why the tourbillon was deemed a chronometric improvement over the basic level escapement, it has remained one of the more difficult complications for any watchmaker to master. Although in more recent times there has been a proliferation of tourbillon escapement watches in various forms, tourbillons were once the preserve of the timekeeping aristocracy of the movement world. Part of the reason lies with the rarity with which tourbillon escapements were entered into the Observatory Competitions (timing competitions measured against observation of planetary movements, reference Chapter 11), and with which they were made available to the consumer; part of the reason lies with the watch being more of a tool than an art form. Tourbillons, when correctly regulated by a master watchmaker/regulator, would win: they were the superior escapement.

With advancements in metal science, precision machining, and in the viscosity and durability of oils for moving parts, it is claimed that the tourbillon is no longer necessary to ensure the same level of chronometric performance as other ordinary escapement watches. However, what independent evidence that does exist offers a contrary view. Tourbillons remain the more accurate escapement mechanism. That said, there are good and bad quality tourbillon watches, and the prospective collector should be aware of what does or does not comprise a tourbillon mechanism.

THE MECHANICS OF THE TOURBILLON

A tourbillon, in its basic state (as conceived by Breguet) aims to counter the external forces acting on the balance wheel, hairspring, and pallet wheel by mounting the escapement in a rotating cage that runs counter to the direction of balance wheel. Usually the rotation is set at 60 seconds (allowing a direct representation with a sub-dial second hand), but there are faster versions (Greubel Forsey have a 24 second rotating tourbillon), and slower versions (Daniel Roth – Jean Daniel Nicolas – have a 2 minute version).

The rotation of the cage counters the external forces on the escapement. The general problem for the mechanical watch is that the very element that regulates the time: The escapement, is the most delicate part of the mechanism. Any outside or exterior forces such as magnetism, large temperature variation, physical shocks as well as gravity can all have an effect on the timekeeping ability of the escapement.

A number of factors that were a concern for Breguet and his contemporaries such as shocks and the ability of metals to cope with variations in temperature have been resolved to a large extent by technological advances in metals: Temperature as a problem has been largely eliminated through advances in metallurgy and understanding how metals and metal alloys expand and contract.

Shocks play less of a role today because of the same advances in metals and the ability to resist an external shock. The escapement is still temporarily deregulated at the time of a shock, but the hairspring does not get deformed as easily as before. There are some watch manufacturers who actually regard the tourbillon mechanism itself as a shock protection mechanism. Richard Mille was renowned for introducing his sports tourbillon watch (the RM001) by throwing it across the room. Likewise, other firms such as Audemars Piguet introduced sports tourbillon watches (the Royal Oak Concept Piece) that could withstand a 500 G-Force shock.

Gravity is the remaining problem and operates through the positional irregularities. Even today, the problem for the watchmaker is to regulate a watch irrespective of the position of the escapement. Although technology has once again allowed improvements, in that timing machines give instantaneous results, positional problems persist for the basic escapement wheel movement. For the basic movement, there are 6 positions over which to time the escapement: Two horizontal (dial up and dial down) and four vertical (crown at 12, 3, 6, and 9 o'clock). The original tourbillon has no effect in the horizontal position as in this state the balance is not affected by gravity as it turns. However, the tourbillon neatly reduces the positional problem to 3 positions: As only one vertical position is required.

Jaeger-LeCoultre Reverso Tourbillon Rose Gold
Photo: Andrew Hildreth

Originally tourbillons were fitted to pocket watches or even carriage clocks (Breguet's first commercial application of the tourbillon was in a carriage clock for Napoleon). In a pocket watch, the tourbillon remained in a vertical position for much of the day and (potentially) night. During the day, a pocket watch sits in the waistcoat pocket; at night on a stand. However, a wristwatch is in a number of positions throughout the day and often moving between vertical and horizontal and all positions in-between. In such circumstances it becomes even more difficult to correctly regulate the escapement as it remains unknown which is the dominant position for the watch throughout the day (mainly horizontal or vertical). Because of such considerations, some watch firms have experimented and started to manufacture multi-axis tourbillons.

DIFFERENT FORMS OF THE TOURBILLON

The last few years have seen a multitude of tourbillons in use. The basic tourbillon (with the cage supported by a bridge top and bottom) has only one axis. It is worth noting that very few are ever submitted for independent verification and hence claims by some that timekeeping for their particular variant of the tourbillon is superior to others is more hyperbole than fact.

Flying tourbillons: (a variant of which is the carrousel tourbillon): rather than being supported by a bridge at the top and bottom of the rotating cage, the flying tourbillon is only supported on one side (usually the base) and is pivot mounted. Such tourbillons have become more popular in recent times as flying tourbillons are designed to be effective at any angle and are hence more suitable for a wristwatch.

Multi-axis tourbillons are still relatively rare on the market as they require considerable skill and research to be effective. Rather than rotate on a single axis, as the ordinary tourbillon does, the tourbillon will rotate through a two or even three. The multi-axis tourbillons are a recent phenomenon and have become possible through improved manufacturing techniques for the component parts. There are still only a handful of watch firms/watchmakers who manufacture such complex escapements.

The double-axis tourbillon was introduced and patented by Anthony Randall in 1977. Although included in a carriage clock, it was Thomas Prescher who managed in 2003 and 2004 to fit such an escapement into a pocket watch and a wristwatch respectively. The double-axis tourbillon, as the name suggests, has the escapement move through both axes over the course of the rotation (usually a minute). Girard Perregaux currently have a version of this tourbillon in production. In 2004, Thomas Prescher managed to also develop a triple-axis tourbillon. This remains a unique achievement.

The double axis tourbillon should be differentiated from a double tourbillon escapement. In 2004 Greubel Forsey introduced a double tourbillon that had the escapement inclined at an angle of 30 degrees to the horizontal, and had the inner cage rotated every minute, and the outer cage rotating every 4 minutes. This was further extended to a quadruple tourbillon by linking two double tourbillons through a differential.

ACCURACY

In recent times, the arguments had been that the tourbillon was an unnecessary complication that simply absorbed energy from the escapement. The improvements in lubrication and in the accuracy of manufacture, coupled with innovations in metal science, had led to escapements that were sufficiently accurate to remove the need for a tourbillon. In particular, use of a Guillaume balance wheel, and with a sufficiently high degree of finish, the watch would prove as accurate as any tourbillon.

Yet, in the competitions that have been held, that have timed watches against each other in the same environment, it has been the tourbillons that have shown to be the more accurate. The very same arguments that could be applied to the basic escapement movements about improving accuracy could also be applied to the tourbillon. In other words, the basic arguments for the tourbillon are probably correct: with all the improvements in lubricants and the ability to machine and finish metal surfaces, the other forces operating on the tourbillon (chiefly gravity) are the primary reason that the tourbillon is more accurate.

The two watch companies that have researched more than any others the forces at play in a tourbillon are Jaeger-LeCoultre and Greubel Forsey. Both have invested substantial resources into the best multi-axis tourbillon watches on the market today. It is worth noting further that Greubel Forsey have (laudably) gone that one step further and actually published the results of their work. With improvements in metal science, it has become possible to manufacture main springs that have a long duration and regular rate of expansion. The increased duration (power reserve) in main springs has allowed for complex forms of the escapement with the necessary power to allow the escapement time to operate.

The tourbillons by Jaeger-LeCoultre and Greubel Forsey are also notable for the simple fact that out of the two modern chronometric competitions that have been held to date, both have taken one of the top prizes in the competition. Hence, they can rightly claim that their tourbillons are the most accurate on the market today. In 2009, Jaeger-LeCoultre claimed the top two prizes for the most accurate wristwatches. Perhaps surprisingly, the single axis tourbillon beat the multi-axis by one point. The Jaeger-LeCoultre Calibre was based on the Jaeger 170 which had won the Geneva Observatory Competition in 1948. In 2011, Greubel Forsey's Double Tourbillon a Technique won first place with a score that was higher than that achieved by the previous competition winner. Arguably, Greubel Forsey can claim to have the most accurate and advanced tourbillon watches on the market.

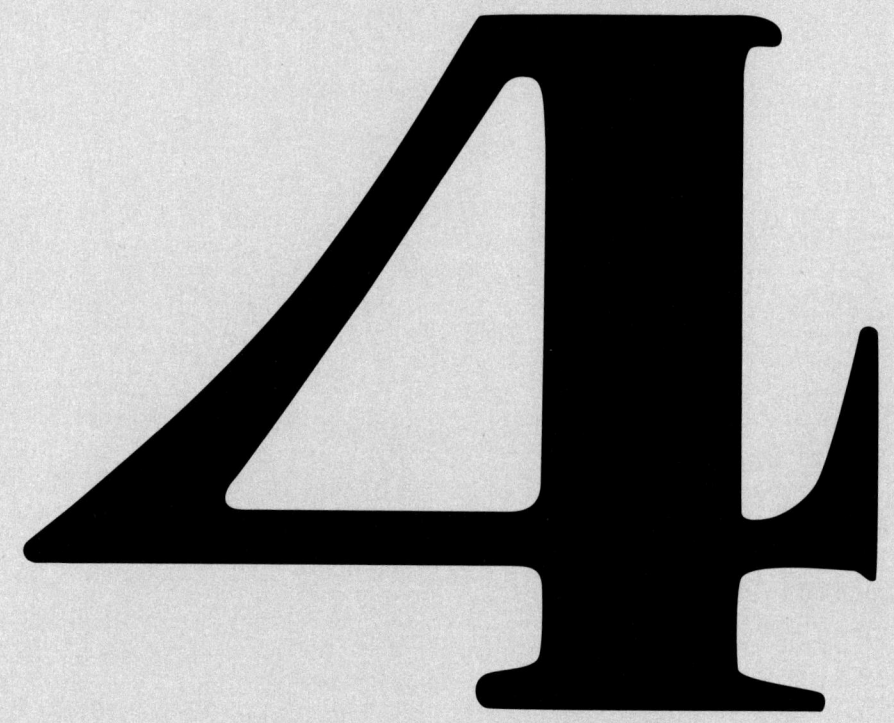

Numeral taken from the dial of a Longines Telemeter Chronograph

LONGEIVITY
PUBLISHER'S INTRODUCTION

Having covered the various possible and intricate aspects of a watch movement in the Complications chapter, it is easy to imagine all the things that could go wrong within a watch. Some value of a timepiece is lost when it loses function or is damaged. It is therefore important to understand how to maintain a watch condition as long as possible. This is not only to keep its condition as close as possible to its watchmaker's original intention, but also to retain its collectible value, which is substantially reduced when parts are damaged or replaced. A watch which is reconditioned badly is no longer the same watch, but, similarly, putting new parts into an old watch will also change it forever. It is important to know what to do, and what not do, to keep the watch in pristine condition from day one.

Historically pocket watches were more protected in breast or waistcoat pockets, hardly exposed other than purely for reading the time. The modern day wristwatch needs to be considerably more sturdy and resilient to withstand the pressures and strains of the everyday watch wearer's wrist.

Sunlight damages dial features, salt water can oxidise metallic parts, abrasions will dent and mark the case, shocks will displace movement parts...

In this chapter we learn a little from Oliver Rapport on the use of watch winders to help maintain a movement, and we transcribe an interview with Jonathan Scatchard on his expert knowledge of antiques and techniques for maintaining longevity.

WATCH WINDING

Oliver Rapport

A mechanical watch is much like a collectible violin or a classic car – it needs to be used regularly to keep it alive. There are also natural elemental effects on watches such as sunlight, seawater, friction and abrasion. These all change the watch's exterior over time. There are of course multiple tricks to keeping expensive items in good condition, and the most important reason for that is to retain the pieces value, not to mention its aesthetic quality. In this chapter we look at simple ways to keep a watch in prime condition and understand the aspects that might deteriorate.

Oliver Rapport, of Rapport London est 1898, tells us a little about watch winders.

Static boxed watch-winders that use clockwise and counter-clockwise rotational motors are often electronically powered and calibrated to the watch in question. Their rotations are designed to imitate the wearer as if he wore an automatic watch during an average day.

An automatic watch has a mechanism that requires regular motion to keep the inner spring constantly charged. This motion is usually provided as it is worn. Once removed from the wrist the stored energy will not run indefinitely, the watch will need to be manually wound and reset eventually.

Many automatic watches have additional features, or 'complications', - date, time, lunar phase, world time etc, so the task of rewinding and recalibrating a watch if it runs down is best avoided.

Rapport Time Arc Duo
Photo: M. A. Rapport & Co. Ltd

Such watches are precision instruments and they actually benefit from exercise – if left unwound for long periods, internal lubricants can be lost from critical areas which will eventually lead to excessive wear on components and subsequent lack of accuracy.

Watch winders have features designed to mimic the action of a watch being worn. The watch is held within its winder at a precise angle while being rotated, and winders can be calibrated to run intermittently in short amounts over long periods of time so that the watch is always permanently wound. They can help a watch to run smoothly for decades extra than if one is not used when the watch is not being worn. The watch winder is the equivalent to the classical violinist, whose job is to maintain the quality of an old Stradivarius Violin (widely known as the most expensive, collectible, musical instruments in the world). Without constant playing, the wood and tone deteriorate much quicker, along with the investment and value.

KEEPING VALUE

Interview with Jonathan Scatchard by Jacob Tomkins

Jonathan Scatchard is an antiques and vintage watch specialist with a website focused on Vintage Heuer. He has particularly focused on early 'pre-Tag Heuer', Rolex and Omega. Drawing on his own book 'How to Value and Compare Wristwatches', we explore some of his experience on longevity and long lasting pieces. We reflect on his thoughts on certain models, and provide some tips and knowledge from his deep, specialist area.

Jonathan explains he has always been a trader, so has only kept a few pieces in a 'collection'. His love for restored old pieces from an era of 'real hardened precision watchmaking', or finding collectible specimens in surprisingly good condition is what fuels his passion and his businesses. "A long lasting piece is only definitely long lasting, once it has lasted a long time!" – The true words of a vintage lover.

JT: What was your first watch?

JS: My first watch was given to me for my 18th birthday – a rectangular Omega Quartz. It was just the coolest thing. You had to use a pen to push the inner crown - ridiculous idea. That was in the early 1980s.
My first mechanical watch a Smiths.

JT: How many times have you serviced them?

JS: The Omega Quartz has been back to Omega once, and it still ticks.
I never had the Smiths serviced at that age, but it would scrub up perfectly.

JT: From a trader's perspective - what are your favourite collection pieces?

JS: I'd have to say Panerai. The early base Marina Panerais...I just love them. It's an important watch to me. Prior to their growth in popularity and before Richemont had taken them over they were relatively unknown, especially in the UK. They used to use Rolex movements, and they were enormous! I had a customer ask in the late 80s if I knew them, which I did, but only for making wrist worn diving instruments and watches for the Italian Military. He asked "Why have they gone and put clocks on straps!??". Little did he know they were to be partly responsible and a central part of the evolving

Left: Zenith el primero auto 01
Right: Heuer Carrera ('pre-Tag) "Panda"
Photo: Vintageheuer.com

fashion of larger watches. When Sylvester Stallone started wearing them in the 90s, they really got noticed.
Otherwise, Heuer – I collected around 60 pieces in my early trading days as they were relatively cheap to me for what they were. I remember Heuer Monacos were 'a fortune' at around £440 when the trade was paying £350 for them.

The Carrera in its early days in the 80s – fantastic collection piece. Also a couple of Breitlings – the Top Time and the early Navitimers with a crown at 9 o'clock. These will all continue to do better and better at retail, so I see their values going up.

JT: What kind of movement needs the least attention?

> JT: Zenith el primero - I don't think I've ever had a serious problem with one. (A chronograph movement that was released in 1969 by Zenith)

JT: Which kind of case material needs the most care/attention?

> JS: Well stainless steel is the way forward. It's the ideal material for watches. Doesn't expand or contract, extremely hard, easy to seal. If you want a sturdy watch, go for an instrument or tool watch (A watch designed specifically for a visual function such as stop watch timing, often with roots in military or engineering)

JT: Which brands are best known for not going wrong?

> JS: Omega have really got it together. Ever since they bought and developed the Coaxial [from George Daniels - reference Chapter 10]. Those movements will be pretty much spot on for 6-10 years.

JT: Which is the most durable movement in your opinion?

> JS: I would hesitate by saying the Heuer Monaco Calibre 11 or 12 – as it has its critics.
> But really it's the Rolex Submariner. You can't fault the movement. They are as hard as rock and so consistent.

JT: What are your thoughts on vintage watches as investments?

> JS: As a collectors activity it's still a very good time to be buying, if not the best. The knowledge is out there and available for everyone now. It was harder to sell vintage in the early days due to lack of information.
> A good clean example of any of the major brands from the 40s/50s onwards is great to put aside. Some Rolex Submariner military issues are selling for £65,000. I was offered them for two decades ago for £1250 each but didn't buy because it would have needed to be for a rare specialist collector, and that was a lot more money then. I've only seen that piece go from strength to strength.

JT: What aspects of condition, if any, affect longevity of value / price?

> JS: Mechanically; most things can be sorted out. If it's running then I have a watchmaker that can sort any other small problems out. I don't buy anything that has seized up. If there is life in it however, that's good. I also always check the bezels to ensure they are not damaged, as you want to avoid replacing them if possible. Original parts, tachymetre and aluminium bezels in unworn

condition are good. Scratched sapphire crystal is not a problem- easy to replace that and new crystals, unlike new dials, don't reduce the value of a piece.

Hands and dial have to be original and not faded. It's VERY difficult to get 'new-old stock' dials so they have to be original and good condition.
If you look at some of the patination on the original Omega Speedmaster dials, you'll see that actually its quite beautiful aging, and this is what collectors love.

Chronographs (stop watches) are very collectible movements but more can go wrong. If a chronograph stops at all then it's a good sign that the watch needs a service, but good chronograph movements should last at least 3-5 years without a service, and with some of the newer oils anything up to seven years.

JT: Give me one watch from the 70s, 80s and 90s that you would buy as a collection/investment piece today, under or around £10k.

JS: Oh I like this question!
1. 1970s - Heuer Monaco 1971 Steve Macqueen Classic blue dial 1133b
2. 1980s - Ebel El Primero Chronograph 1982 Rose Gold Black Dial 1911 - Used in Miami Vice and a super cool, reliable chronograph. They can be picked up for not a huge sum, quality is exceptional and they are iconic.
3. 1990s – a simple Panerai Luminor PVD Date, designed as it was in the 40s

Jonathan is a believer in spreading industry knowledge to help collectors form long lasting and valuable collections. He will be contributing to the Twelve Journal website and hard copies with further insight into vintage pieces and other collectibles.

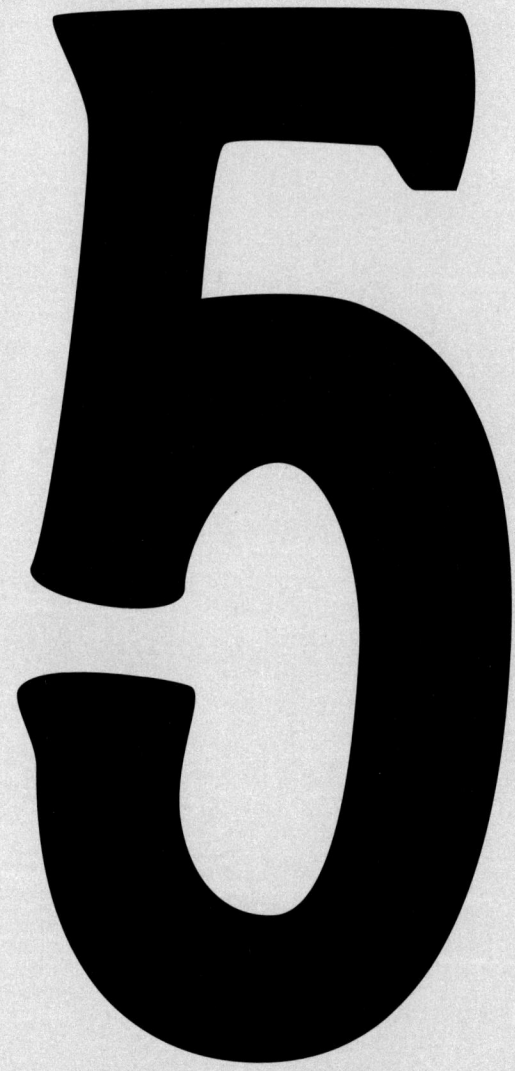

Numeral taken from the dial of a Vacheron Constantin 1972

MATERIALS
PUBLISHERS' INTRODUCTION

The use of materials has been a central area of experimentation and research by watchmakers since the dawn of horology. In an attempt to reduce fluctuations in time keeping, improve temperature resilience, increase shock absorption, even enhance attractiveness, many materials have been explored. Today we see watchmakers using composites found in aerospace, or spring systems used in formula one pistons, to give additional improvements to watch designs, both inside the movement and out.

Most movements are only made possible using specialist inert metals, for example, an average balance wheel that vibrates (rotates) 28,800 times per hour, regulating the expansion and contraction of the hair spring, needs to be made of a material which will not thermally expand or contract, or create a magnetic fluctuation in the movement around it. Charles Edouard Guillame invented an early successful, and Nobel prize winning, version of this mechanism part in 1896 using a nickel steel alloy.

It is also the case that harder metals are easier to keep in good condition, and through using the right methods, all materials can be maintained to a high level.

In this chapter we explore the past and some turning points for materials used in watchmaking. We try to understand the relevance and reasons for application of such materials, from a frivolous diamond setting in an 18kt pink gold watch, to the use of manufactured rubies and jewels, so crucial to the workings of a watch movement.

MATERIALS

Jacob Tomkins

Although watches are now a luxury product, they once chiefly represented the latest in technological advance. They were made by technical geniuses of their time, who spared no expense in the materials used. The more durable and cheaper materials such as steel only became common later. This article covers the developments in use of materials in the cases, movements and watch dials.

High quality materials are central to accurate timekeeping. Horologists have always competed to find the best materials to combat gravitational effect, temperature change and power loss – the main culprits in time inaccuracy. Many times in the history of mechanical clocks and watches, alternate materials enabled discovery of solutions to battling time discrepancy. Research into the materials and the cost of those parts themselves prove to be a greater cost to the manufacturer than the watch buyer may think. This relates back to understanding the value and cost discussion in Chapter 1. Only the best will do; such is the history and heritage of industry. Watchmakers have always demanded the most advanced technologies, talented experts and deliberately chosen materials.

Early clocks that stood in hallways and receptions of buildings of the 1600-1800s were made of wood, with copper, brass and iron used as the main materials. Gold was used only for decoration, until it was realized that the inertia of the precious metals lent consistencies that were not achievable with other metals of the time. Silver was the favourite material of the pocket watchmaker, as it was easily beaten, moulded and engraved, and relatively inexpensive as a jewellery material. Pocket watches were also significantly more protected and well looked after objects than the modern wristwatch – spending most of their lives in the breast pockets of the wealthy few. But silver and gold pocket watches were not designed as sturdy, reliable mechanisms and would often stop working. The early watchmakers' problem was how to make a watch they did not have to keep on fixing! After all, watchmakers were popular and needed their time to make new products for new clients. This led to a fascination with materials and extensive development by the early, organised brands into smaller, compact, harder wearing movements and watches. A famous example is in 1931 when Jaeger-LeCoultre first created the Reverso – a watch that could be flipped around on the wrist to reveal a protective solid metal caseback. Designed for polo playing military men, and housing a tiny, sturdy, rectangular calibre movement made in-house, of course, by Jaeger-LeCoultre, this was a groundbreaking addition to the world of watches. It is also a watch that has hardly changed in appearance or function since before collecting was so popular. The Reverso range still contains some of the most collectible watches available.

The most common materials in watchmaking are by far steel and gold. Steel, however, is not inert like precious metals such as gold, and contains traces and in some cases high percentages of nickel. Silicon and aluminium can also be found in steel. A disadvantage is that nickel can cause allergic reactions – 15% of women suffer from some level of nickel allergy.

Linde Werdelin Spidolite Anthracide DLC
Photo: Linde Werdel

Steel became the favourite watchmaking material mainly for military purposes in the early 1900s, and it has remained so until today. Its properties are attractive – hard, workable, attractive, maintainable, light, stiff, and almost inert. However, adventurous brands now experiment with any material that carries some value and interesting properties: carbon fibre, titanium, ceramics, aluminium, toughened zirconia, sapphire crystal, composite kevlars – with examples by brands such as Richard Mille, Linde Werdelin, Urwerk, MB&F, Romain Jerome or HYT. You will discover some innovations focused entirely around materials. Fascinating mixes of industrial engineering, CAD design, chemical science and horology mix together in these brands' proudest creations.

Coatings for metals have become widely used in watch manufacturing, and a popular process borrowed from the military and medical industries is Physcial Vapour Deposition ('PVD'). The process uses a vacuum chamber to bond a superfine molecular coating to the top layer of the material. These coatings help to combat many problems with common watchmaking materials, namely lubrication issues, reducing chances of allergic reactions, and scratch resistance on exterior surfaces. The coatings come in a range of consistency and colour, most frequently seen in black or dark grey. Black PVD coated watches have always been functional for hunting or military use, but are currently fashionable, so are produced by the majority of brands. The advances in the coatings industry means it can now be economically viable and relatively reliable as a mass product process, whereas even recently, it was "more of an art than a science" (Prof. Tony Anson, Biomaterials and Biomechanics, Brunel University).

The aesthetic benefits of having a black watch are of course slightly lost on gold watches, as the display of wealth is then lost (important for some), but it is a very widely used process on steel, and especially titanium to which it adheres well.
Coatings come in many incarnations. Plasma coating such as Diamond Like Carbon ('DLC') is increasing in popularity due to its unequaled hardness. It is an unnatural molecular carbon dust with a similar hardness to natural diamond. It is introduced to watch parts in a controlled laboratory environment similar to PVD. The manufactured diamond molecule encrusts itself, changing the colour and hardness of the surface of the metal, protecting the coated steel and offering a different look – thus changing the appearance and impression of the watch. This has already had an impact on watch styling. The industry has generally avoided colouring exteriors of watches largely due to previously limited ranges of solutions such as soft paints and electro plating methods, unable to withstand the wear and tear of an everyday watch.

While coatings provide perfect durability for everyday time pieces, they also have been widely used in industrial functions as a lubricant in heavy, complex machinery. There is almost no friction between two surfaces sporting a DLC coating, so mechanical moving parts benefit from less oil or other lubricants. Recently, therefore, some of the more adventurous watch brands have embarked upon using coated parts inside the movement as well. This harks back to the original uses of the coatings for lubrication and shows the industry is now taking the coatings more seriously as a potentially worthwhile addition in terms of longevity of the time piece, and of course more accurate time keeping.

Top: Richard Mille RM0027 'Nadal' with DLC Coating
Photo: Andrew Hildreth

Bottom: Panerai Radiomir Black Seal PVD ref PAM 00292
Photo: Watchclub/Michal Solarski

EVOLUTION
OF THE
INDEPENDENT WATCH BRAND

Luke Waite

Another side to the watch industry that takes a serious, innovative and bold approach to new materials for purposes of modification and aesthetics are the independent retailers and brands. These new emerging brands that work with existing market products, such as Bamford and Sons, Prohunter and Titan Black, have seen significant growth in recent years due to the internet and a thriving aftermarket.

Luke Waite, owner of Titan Black (bespoke watch coating and modifications brand), gives us some insightful commentary about the challenges associated with entering the market with two core passions; satisfying the customer desires and unique methods of using and handling materials.

Titan Black 'Bolt' - customised Rolex Green Glass Milgauss
Photo: Titan Black

Top: Titan Black 'Avatar' customised Role Daytona
Bottom: Titan Black Azure' - customised Rolex Yachmaster II
Photos: Titan Black

Occasionally it is important to view the present through the lens of the past, which allows for a different perspective and also acts as a reminder of progress. It was not so long ago that the difficult economic environment that consumed the world, contributed to a rise in costs and a reduction in clients throughout virtually all consumer sectors.

For any ambitious entrepreneur or visionary, the notion of entering into the luxury wristwatch market as a start-up independent watch brand has always been at best a daunting prospect, let alone in the height of a global recession. But it was Sir Frederick Henry Royce (Co-Founder of Rolls Royce) who inspired me when he said: 'Strive for perfection in everything you do. Take the best that exists and make it better. When it does not exist, design it'.

The luxury market is now defined by what the customers' desires and aspirations, not what brands dictate. I have always felt that the moment your ideas are abandoned, it is time for change. So who better to take note than the customers themselves? This is not to say that the brands are doing anything wrong - far from it. They hold the mastery and craftsmanship that have pioneered some of the most sophisticated watch complications previously thought impossible.

But ultimately this does not determine a brand's success, it is the client who ultimately controls the market and their patronage/loyalty is what all brands seek.

My experience in dealing with important collectors, who acquire modern watches as part of their investment portfolios, has proved to be a minefield with no magical algorithm to guarantee success. It's clear, increasingly so, that some customers are choosing their brand loyalty based on function and aesthetics, and as such customisation companies evolved as a result of this service not yet being offered by the established watch houses.

It would be folly to suggest that with seven billion people in the world, everyone's desires are catered for. Thus began my own interface for the clients, instilling the concept that they can create what they imagine, bringing the combination of their watch passion and their imagination to life. Allowing customers to be involved in a modification or a design process, using digital or online design programs, brought the process of buying a watch closer to that of creating a piece of jewellery with a jeweler, or indeed how watches would have been made to order in their early days.

With none of the main brands able to facilitate the changes to products I've desired for customers, finding and working with the correct aftermarket craftsmen became an art form in itself. I spent years hand picking experts that had not already been headhunted. To translate and communicate and vision between a customer and a watchmaking artisan is a painstaking process. Establishing a team of master watchmakers, machinists, engravers, dial artisans, graphic designers and watch enthusiasts were some of the ingredients to drive my team...

There are many aspects to this micro engineering exercise, the most dominant force within the customisation process being the DLC or Diamond-Like Carbon coating. The DLC industry is more commonly associated with the aerospace, military, automotive and medical sectors. The entrance of wristwatches to this list meant the recalibration of existing machinery and the re-educating of engineers not familiar with the aesthetic levels of scrutiny demanded by the sophisticated luxury watch buyer. The fact that we have used five factories in as many countries in as many years tells it's own story of the challenges in our processes. When I finally found the UK's authority on plasma-assisted chemical vapour deposition (PACVD) technology, I was able to define and develop the ideal coating for customisations on these wonderful and extraordinary micro-engineered collectibles.

In their laboratory a crew of specialists give the watches their DLC treatment of (PACVD – Plasma Assisted Chemical Vapour Deposition). The watch is carefully taken apart and ultrasonically cleaned of any dirt, grease and fingerprints. The metal watch parts to be treated (in any combination of the case, bracelet, bezel, crown, clasp etc.) are placed into a vacuum chamber, where they are negatively charged and exposed to positively-ionised carbon plasma. The microscopic carbon particles bond perfectly to any area of the surface of the watch parts that can be reached by air, leaving them impeccably even and smooth. The watch surface is now up to eight times harder than steel. After the DLC application process, which takes around four to five hours, the watches are reassembled and tested again for quality and accuracy before arriving with their owners (quality and accuracy are rarely effected by the coating but the testing process is treated just like the watches' first assembly). The ideal result doesn't depend on the age of the watch, and so this customisation transcends the age of a watch and can be applied to nearly any metal, with steel and titanium being the best for adherence.

Finding dial artisans who were able to work with modern graphic artists proved to be the most difficult stage in the process of modifying a watch. They possess by far the most specific skill set within a production chain that involves generations of experience to coordinate certain transformations. Needless to say blending modern designs with master craftsmanship is not without its complications. Taking an already perfect piece of engineering and changing its aesthetics without fundamentally altering its DNA is a delicate but imperative process. It ensures the connection between its rich heritage provided by the brands and the evolution into its present day state.

Project timing has an intrinsic role when managing the expectations of passionate clients, used to impeccable levels of service. One mistake could put a reputation of dedication to a service in question. Brand image and reputation has never been more scrutinised through social feeds and blogs, and combining exceptional quality with timely delivery is crucial to a luxury brands survival. When you have a great watch product, you have some of the best customers in the world.

In the end you are only as good as your product and being able to stand by it in this market is gratifying. The feeling of accomplishment after delivering to the client exactly what they desire is rewarding for all involved. Undoubtedly it is this deep connection and understanding between the brand and the client that will determine the next phase of the brand's success. This in turn will effect sales across the market of the original unmodified pieces. Because of this gratification and apparent success of close relationships with customers I will always continue to develop my customisations around my customers dreams.

Greubel Forsey Double Tourbillon 30° Edition Histrorique
Rose Gold (left - original, right - 'Anthracite' dial)
Photo: Andrew HIldreth

Numeral taken from the dial of a Panerai

MODERN DAY MANUFACTURING
PUBLISHER'S INTRODUCTION

Our previous chapter on materials naturally leads us to questions about the production and manufacturing of watches. For example, gold is significantly more expensive than steel , but anyone with a knowledge of metals knows it is more labour intensive and resource-consuming to manufacture intricate objects in steel than gold. It follows that steel should more expensive in the watch retail environment than gold. This is quite rightly the case with titanium, which commands higher prices than gold in some watches, but you would not pay more for a gram of titanium than you would for a gram of gold.

Manufacturing has changed altogether with the introduction of digital tools and technology aided scientific experimentation.

In this chapter we discuss how the design process leading up to manufacturing has changed for watch designers and brands, and we also look at some benefits and disadvantages of certain materials. We have given examples of newer brands which are gaining popularity because of the non-traditional concepts and methods used in their manufacturing, to help readers understand why the unusual to the traditional industry is so interesting.

MODERN
MANUFACTURING AND DESIGN
IN WATCHES

Jacob Tomkins

Modern manufacturing has driven the miniaturisation of almost everything we use. Thankfully, watches are an exception to this rule, as they have not become much smaller since their first incarnations. Advance in manufacturing has provided significant stimulation to the evolution of watch design. Where pen and ink were once the medium to sketch designs for jewelers to craft the metals, now industrial designers and product experts are able to collaborate to combine multiple fields of expertise into the design of watches. The intricacy and depth of engineering in watch cases can be as complex as manufacturing the body of a car – certainly you can find similarities in the number of parts and stages in the process. Computer automated design (CAD) has helped to evolve the design and concept stages of watch making significantly. Twenty-five years ago the only way to see if an idea worked or looked good was to make it. Now one can create endless variations and revisions of design, and even simulate the mechanical processes to visualize the behaviour of a watch and moving parts, as pixels on a screen.

This has meant that the design influences on watches have stretched far beyond the imagination of just horologists, jewellers and watchmakers. We regularly see imitations or repetitions from other industrial applications in watches, such as automotive or nautical themes or functions, for example the famous Hublot porter hole bezel most often seen on the Big Bang collection; the incorporation of the patented Martin Baker shock absorption technology from ejector seats that Bremont have now used in their movements, as well as their crowns commonly exhibiting a subtle etching of a rotor from a WWII spitfire plane; IWC have always been famous for their fighter plane cockpit dials imitating the devices actually used by pilots; DeWitt for their propeller dial chronographs and Romain Jerome for their articulated shoulder lugs on their Moon Invader. These imitations are almost purely cosmetic today, but are echoes of previous required functions in other sectors and sources of inspiration in watchmaking.

Military influence is evident in watchmaking history not only because timepieces played an all-important part in precision during combat and travel, but also because it was a reliable and well funded industry responsible for considerable advances in all technologies. This meant many wartime manufacturing brands were supported by European armies, which produced reliably functional relevant designs. The

Richard Mille RM055 'Bubba Watson', case made from a
new composite; white aluminium-toughened zirconia
Photo: Andrew Hildreth

watch industry only needed to miniaturise some of the original concepts to create extra complications and functions, and the style of exterior design grew with these functions, giving life to a huge 'military watch' arena.

Gold and silver were used almost exclusively in the watchmaking industry for some time, although they are not necessarily practical materials for a durable watch. As watches have become less a luxury and more workaday, with the cost of movement manufacture significantly dropping, the cost of 50-100g of gold (roughly the weight of an average gold watch case) relative to the cost to manufacture, is very high. It became more common among brands to encase simpler movements and more affordable ranges in less expensive materials, hence the widespread availability of steel watches. Almost all watch brands today will have steel and gold versions of the same models, in an effort to be accessible to a wider range of buyers; some people prefer, and can afford, to own a gold watch rather than its steel counterpart. These usually will have a lower production count but might be more in demand. A drawback of a lower cost material such as stainless steel is that the material contains nickel, which can cause allergic reaction, especially among women. This can be counteracted by a thin molecular carbon coating on the watch, or in Rolex's case using a stainless steel with such a low nickel content that it becomes negligible. Fine watches such as grand complications and specialty tourbillions will almost always be cased in a precious metal such as gold or platinum. Regularly these watches command around £1m due to their rarity, horological proficiency and provenance, rendering the cost of the gold or platinum irrelevant.

Automatic watches stimulated a need for – and then a fashion for – bigger cases, needing room for the rotor and to show off design features or the subject of inspiration in the time piece's case. Notable brands like Hublot and Audemars Piguet have exploited the trend in high quality fashion, with their extensive Big Bang and Royal Oak Offshore series respectively. But many traditional manufacturers such as Patek Philippe still pride themselves on producing a greater number of thinner, more elegant manual wind watches.
Gerald Genta, 1931-2011, one of the most influential watch designers of the last century, helped to make steel a more widely used material in fine watchmaking. In the early 1970s he was drafted in by Audemars Piguet to save the company from a potentially damaging financial downturn – a situation shared by many luxury Swiss watch brands at the time, mainly due to the catastrophically successful introduction of the Quartz movement from Japan. Genta designed the Royal Oak ref. 5402, which was the first elegant luxury automatic sports watch, with an integrated steel bracelet and a revolutionary angular bezel and dial design.
It was immensely popular, and helped to steer buyers back towards the glory of hand manufactured mechanical Swiss watches, away from their modern digital cousins.

Linde Werdelin is a brand currently sprinting into the limelight, with two ranges of watches aimed at ski and diving enthusiasts. Their design is unusual, robust and almost futuristic. But their build quality is where they become most impressive.
Their latest cases include rich combinations of steel, sapphire and titanium, coated in an ultra-tough black diamond coating. They are even venturing into the carbon composite arena, combining an in-house metal alloy they call ALW (Alloy Linde Werdelin) and an outer shock absorbing, unmistakable case of forged carbon. They have launched their own movement this year, with their first complication – a moon phase – giving a display of the moon in its current position.

Linde Werdelin are versatile, modern and creative with their design and use of materials. They produce a reassuringly low number of pieces every year (under 5000). A feature which makes this brand so unusual, is their various 'instruments' to go with their watches. If you're a skier, it's the 'Rock' – to deliver information on your altitude and outside temperature. If you're a diver, it's the 'Reef' – 'the worlds most sophisticated dive computer '. Both these digital devices sport anodised aluminium cases and sapphire crystal screens, recording your whole sporting experience to feed your data in your own chosen format. Forward thinking design and integratable lifestyle products – is this where watches are going?

Romain Jerome have manufactured watches like the Titanic-DNA and the Moon- DNA using metals from the Titanic and elements recovered from the Moon. Dewitt have manufactured concept watches such as the Antipode, a grande complication that rotates inside out and upside down in its case axis, sporting grand complications, minute repeater, two dials and a staggering list of parts and materials. Their other concept watch is the enormous but very lightweight WX-1. This has a 21-day power reserve which sits as comfortably on your wrist as a tea-pot, but looks sensational, especially mounted in its desk clock configuration. Returning to essentials, a watch needs to tell the time, encapsulate the love and interest of its owner, and fit on a wrist. Manufacturing processes will help evolve the market and provide great interest to enthusiasts for all time to come, so long as the market continues to innovate as technology changes. Horology will always be at the heart of a watch, and I believe we are only just at the dawn of a new era of technologically minded horological machines. Mechanical objects with modern brains, perhaps. A young designer at Seiko spent 28 years developing the Spring Drive movement, which was released in 2005 - a mechanical watch with a microelectronic regulator and an accuracy of one second per day. Is this an example of what we can expect to see in the Swiss Manufacturing future? It is certainly a contender for one of the best time keepers around.

Numeral taken from the dial of an A. Lange & Soehne
gold hunting cased chronograph

HOW TO COLLECT
INTRODUCTION

Ken Kessler takes over in this chapter to give us some deep insight into his own collecting knowledge, and some guidance for those who want to expand on their own

Considering that wristwatch collecting has only been an identifiable subculture for around 25 years, it has grown rapidly into a mature field with all the sources needed to make the novice feel comfortable and the veteran feel respected. Prior to the first wristwatch-only auctions of the late 1980s, collecting timekeepers meant only clocks and pocket watches. Now, the wristwatch rules. In the second decade of the 21st Century, London alone can provide you with at least a dozen serious vintage watch specialists, while the book world is awash with price guides and brand histories. The only things lost along the way are the mystique and the adventure: gone are the days when an estate auction or a charity shop would yield watch treasures for pocket change. Now, you can find any collectible on line, however rare, provided you're prepared to pay for it.

If you're new to the field, stick to a few simple guidelines and you'll never feel overwhelmed or, worse, cheated. First, decide what watches interest you, e.g. military models or diving watches. Focus on those and don't be distracted – same advice one would give to any type of collector. Second, buy watches only from specialists if you want to avoid fakes and have the security of a warrantee. Buying on-line or at auction demands a bit more experience. Specialists like the Watch Club, David Duggan and Somlo Antiques eliminate doubt.

Lastly, the most important advice you will ever be given: only buy watches you like, that you'll actually wear. Otherwise, you're better off giving the money to charity.

FORM AND FUNCTION

Ken Kessler

Bauhaus sensibilities have long informed the design of watches, even before Bauhaus existed. In the earliest timepiece recognised as a modern wristwatch – the watch Louis Cartier produced for Santos-Dumont – function dictated the form.

Wristwatches were never treated solely as tools or precision instruments, even in the early days: they have always overlapped with jewellery, for they are decorative. As has long been recognised, they are the only form of jewellery most men find suitable as a means of expression beyond a ring. But as has been seen during the past decade, thanks to the efforts of Hublot, Jacob & Co and others, restraint is a thing of the past.

For a collector, such a quality might seem horrific, and I will never forget the general reaction among Paneristi to Panerai's application of diamonds to the numerals on a Radiomir. Taste, however, is subjective, and that monstrosity is now highly coveted and collectible, like that other, even more extreme monument to vulgarity, the leopard-skin Rolex Daytona.

Back in the world of good taste (however much that smacks of snobbery), the all-time greats are exemplars of functionality. The aforementioned Cartier Santos and its sibling born a few years later, the Tank, tell only the time, in square or rectangular cases, but they do so in a manner that has allowed both to survive a century or more in production, with few changes to the basic ingredients.

Both have grown in size, according to the tastes of the modern age. Both have been graced with complications, adorned with gems, and been fitted with straps or bracelets, but even the most extreme variant – the Santos 100 with black rubber details – remains unmistakeably a descendant of the watch commissioned by a pioneering pilot so he would not have to take his hands off the joystick to extract a watch from his pocket.

While the Cartier Tank – the more famous of the two – has never been out of fashion, its reputation of late has inexplicably been on the rise. Seemingly overnight, values of second-hand models have shot up, but the collector must be wary: Cartier Tanks are a genre unto themselves.

Top: Cartier Tank Vintage Louis
Bottom: Cartier Tank Vintage White Gold
Photos: Watchclub/Michal Solarski

I once saw a tray of about fifteen Tanks in a specialist shop in London, one of peerless repute. To the untrained observer, they all looked pretty much the same, all in superlative condition, all in yellow gold on identical black crocodile straps. The price variations, due to the movements within, the type of dial and other considerations, produced a price span of £2000 to £35,000. And, no, I did not know which was which.

Of the functions that forced themselves upon forms, the most widespread for collector popularity as well as usefulness are multiple time-zone (a.k.a. 'world traveller') watches and diving watches. But even within those categories, the means of realising the function can result in widely varying solutions. The world-traveller is a perfect example of this.

When Louis Cottier created his watches in the 1930s to show all of the world's time zones at once, the ideal solution was to arrange the names of key cities, one per time zone, around the dial. With deft use of the hand-setting, the owner could observe local time and home time, while all of the other zones were in their correct position by design. So, if you were in New York, and your home time was London, the position of the cities showed Paris one hour ahead.

Patek Philippe embraced the Cottier design, creating models with enamelled world maps in the centre – a touch of style to enhance that ring of names. They now rank among the most valuable of all vintage Pateks. Tissot chose instead to array the names of the cities like the spokes in a wheel, and that treasure from the 1950s, too, is escalating in value, if still affordable.

Even when reducing the coverage to two or three time zones, it was possible to devise differing solutions. Rolex's GMT-Master of 1954 and Glycine's Airman of 1953 use 24-hour hands in conjunction with 12-hour hands, augmented by rotating bezels, to allow the user to set home and destination with ease, but the eye can be thrown by a 24-hour hand, for which noon can look like 6 o'clock. But neither model would be mistaken for the other, even though both place the same function over form.

One could say the same about diving watches, comparing Blancpain's Fifty Fathoms to Rolex's Submariner – again, both born close together – while only the psychedelic Sixties could have delivered unto us the orange-dialled Doxa Sub300T, so coloured for improved legibility in the water. It also proves that the designer can intend to do nothing more than improve the functionality of a watch, while inadvertently gracing it with a hint of bling.

COLLECTING BY MAKER

Ken Kessler

As a default theme, there's none better than collecting watches by manufacturer. It's almost too obvious to be worth highlighting. Think about it: when was the last time a fellow-collector said to you that he (it's always a he) accumulates diving watches, or chronographs, or triple calendars. Never – that's when. It's usually "I'm a Rolex collector" or "I'm a Paneristo."

See where I'm going with this? They even have there own nicknames for the watches. Rolex enthusiasts speak of "Double Reds" and "Jean-Claude Killys". Patek Philippe enthusiasts only speak in model numbers, as in, "Did you see the rose gold 1463 they had at Bonham's?" Cartier Tank fetishists argue about movements – EWC? Jaeger? (Possibly the same thing, actually…) And so it goes.

There is a certain beauty, though, in collecting by marque because – if the brand has longevity and therefore a big enough past catalogue to explore – it provides incredible focus. Auction catalogues no longer overwhelm. You skate past the other brands. There is a finite element to your collecting lust.

Not so if you collect, say, diving watches and are cursed with a completist mentality. It's easier to name brands that don't make diving watches than even to try to list all the ones that do. And you could go broke just collecting all the various Rolex Submariners. Which brings us back to collecting by brand.

If the company has been around for, say, a century, and it produces watches in a number of categories, you then can narrow down the collecting to a specific series, or type of watch. The most likely to appeal to you would be watches within their catalogues that address your other pursuits.

You may be a suave soul who never dresses down. Thus you might have a passion for Piaget's ultra-thin dress watches. You're outdoorsy, with an equestrian tendency, so Hermés would be a natural target. A yachtsman? IWC, Panerai, Audemars-Piguet and Corum are but a few that would appeal to your nautical bent. And if you're a car fanatic, the field is even wider: TAG-Heuer's models named after racing circuits, Breitling serves Bentley owners, Aston-Martin has collaborated on models with Jaeger-LeCoultre … there's a book just waiting to be written on the car/watch link.

Piaget Altiplano Platinum
Photograph: Andrew Hildreth

Which brand you choose – for whatever reason – will have undeniable impact on your adventures as a collector. Some brands enjoy territorial cults: Hamilton is huge among collectors in the USA, Smiths has followers in the UK, Germans love IWC, Italians do strange things for Rolexes. But a global hierarchy exists, and the impact it has on collectors is down to pricing.

There is no better example of the Law of Supply and Demand than a collectors' market. One can name sublime wine producers making fewer than 2000 cases per year – which is small production – yet the prices will never match Bordeaux or Burgundies in quantities 100 times that, simply because there are more collectors for the latter. So, too with watches.

In watch collecting, there is no doubt whatsoever that the high end for collectors consists of Patek Philippe complications. Usually, in any given year, nine of the ten highest bids in auction were Pateks. The second most sought-after line is Rolex, with prices escalating every year, the insanity initiated by Italian collectors. After that, there's a free-for-all among collectors of Audemars-Piguet, Cartier, Vacheron Constantin, Breitling, Heuer (pre-TAG), Omega and Longines. The newest brand to drive enthusiasts crazy is Panerai, which has risen faster in prestige than any watch brand one can name.

In every case, the prices are elevated as much by the sheer number of collectors who are fter the same pieces as they are by rarity. Combine the two – an ultra-rare Rolex or a one-off Patek Philippe – and the prices skyrocket. What that means, though, is that the canny collector stays away from the obvious makes.

For an analogy, instead of getting your butt kicked by a Chinese billionaire at a wine auction, one who simply will not leave without that Petrus vertical, look to something just as delicious, like Masseto. Don't collect Ferraris; collect Stanguellinis. In watches, you can get the same movement found in a Rolex Cosmograph in dozens of other models. I have a Gallet and a Universal Geneve, both powered by the Valjoux 72. Their combined price is 1/10th that of a Cosmograph. And their rarity makes them far cooler.

I'll leave you with this illustration, as you think about a brand worthy of your attention. After you've studied the brand's history and found out that it won more awards and made more calibres than anyone else, you might figure that Longines is the one to collect. You may value individualism above other qualities, so you'll choose, say, Vacheron over Patek because the former has made far fewer watches than the latter.

To insert this into the world of the collector, when a bunch of guys compare timepieces over cigars and brandy – now more common than you'd think – picture a dinner I attended 15 years ago in Paris. Eight friends of longstanding, united by a common industry but not watch-related. A funky restaurant, wine flowing, great conversation. But eight strongly individualistic personalities. On their wrists? One vintage Rolex, and seven Panerais.

I then understood why women go ballistic if two of them turn up at the same event in the same dress. You have been advised.

10 BOOKS
FOR COLLECTORS

Ken Kessler

Whatever you collect – wine, cars, cameras or, yes, wristwatches – you need to acquire enough knowledge to ensure that the pursuit is fulfilling. Not only in the sense of acquisition: that goes without saying, because acquiring the targets of your lust is collecting's raison d'être and main challenge. It is but a part of the experience.

Seasoned collectors will tell you that much of the joy derived from collecting involves meeting other enthusiasts, sharing knowledge and lore, swapping tales of great finds and 'the ones that got away.' To facilitate this, to enhance your knowledge and, as a result, to increase your success in locating the timepieces you covet, a basic library of books about watches will prove invaluable. Think 'pub quiz readiness.'

You will notice this list of 10 great 'reads' for watch enthusiasts includes only one price guide, but that's because nearly half of it has nothing to do with watch values: the price guide recommended here includes a crash course in watch collecting. Due to the nature of the market, price guides are obsolete before they're printed. If it's values you want, keep your eye on auction results, eBay and selling sites.

Equally, there are no single-make histories here: you will only buy single brand histories related directly to the makes that interest you. Instead, the titles below aim to do one thing: increase your general knowledge of the objects you love so much.

The Watch Buff's Book of Trivia

by Norma Buchanan
ISBN 0-9772512-0-9. $13.95

Sometimes, you have to lighten up about your passion. Norma Buchanan, as serious a journalist as you will ever meet, let down her hair for this entertaining diversion, subtitled '465 Fun Facts About Timepieces'. Buchanan, a contributing editor at US magazine WatchTime, has collected a vast amount of trivia guaranteed to amuse even a room full of po-faced Patek obsessives who usually converse only in four-digit numbers. From the French author who mentioned Breguets in three novels to the make of watch stolen from Prince Charles, this is a tonic for anyone who wants non-watch enthusiasts to be charmed into our hobby.

Masters Of Contemporary

Michael Clerizo
ISBN 978 0 500 514856. £55

We are nearly 25 years into an era that saw the emergence of a generation of bold and inventive designers who have revolutionised the watch world. Their timepieces are expensive, rare and eminently collectible. Most of us, though, know nothing more about them than what we find in their catalogues. Michael Clerizo enabled a number of them to state their cases in their own words. George Daniels, Svend Andersen, Philippe Dufour, Franck Muller, Vianney Halter, Roger Smith and many other auteurs are revealed through text that is fascinating, acerbic, contentious and – more importantly – entertaining. For those who have never met these legendary watchmakers, this is a perfect introduction.

George Daniels - A Master Watchmaker

by Michael Clerizo
ISBN 978-0-500-51636-2. £75.

Once you've absorbed Clerizo's sublime Masters of Contemporary Watchmaking, this 'catalogue raisonné' of George Daniels' complete works lets you know who was the 'daddy' of 20th Century watchmaking. Clerizo worked with him, up to Daniels' death in 2011. The first watchmaker to create everything needed to construct a timepiece, Daniels created 25 pocket watches from raw materials, using period tools. He chronicled the work of Breguet and nurtured the estimable Roger W. Smith. He married the traditional skills he wished to prevent from dying out and invented the Co-axial Escapement adopted by Omega – arguably his greatest achievement. Clerizo has gathered it all into one gorgeous tome that will leave you dazzled.

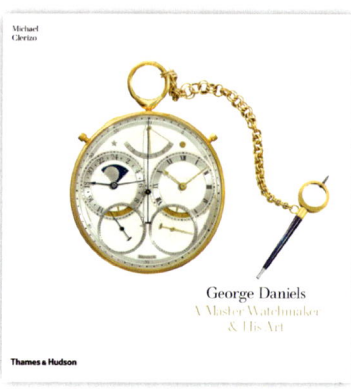

Marking Time

by Michael Korda
ISBN 0-7607-3576-X. US $14.95

Collector Korda is the editor-in-chief of Simon & Schuster and the author of more than a dozen titles, so here we have a watch book as readable as a novel. Sub-titled Collecting Watches – and Thinking About Time, it explores the how and why of watch-collecting without being dry, densely fact-laden or blindly preachy. Watch lore and common sense, autobiographical anecdotes, musing on the nature of time, the mind of the collector, the romance of watches and the mystery of previous owners: it is 'unputdownable' if you love watches. Marking Time is erudite, entertaining, elegant and educational – the 'nicest' watch-related book I've read since Longitude.

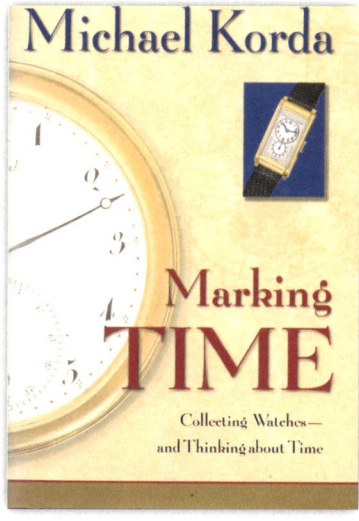

Longitude

by Dava Sobel
ISBN 1-85702-502-4. £12

Proof that a book about watch development can be a bestseller. The information above refers to the hardback edition of 1995 – since then, it's been issued as a paperback, as a deluxe illustrated edition and inspired at least three TV docu-dramas. By now, everyone knows the story of how John Harrison had to fight the establishment to prove he had devised a clock accurate enough to determine longitude – thus saving sailors' lives for the past couple of centuries. 2014 is the 300th anniversary of Parliament passing the Longitude Act, which offered the victor the enormous sum of £20,0

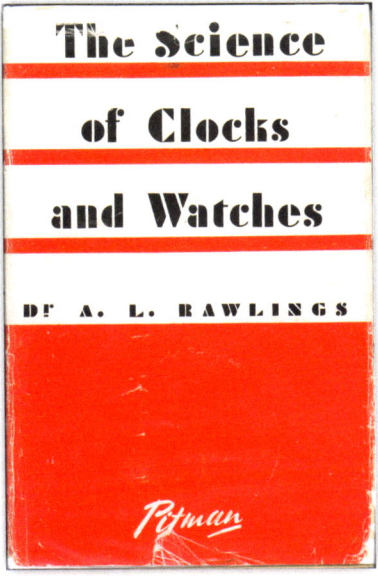

The Science of Clocks and Watches

by Dr. A.L. Rawlings
No ISBN, out of print.

This isn't meant to antagonise you, but to inspire you to find a copy. If, like me, you have no watchmaking skills, but wish to know how watches work, this 65-year-old volume will prove to be the equivalent of Mr. Chips. Plain English, no need for the reader to possess a degree in physics nor mathematics – it is simply a lucid discourse on how timekeepers work. Yes, it predates key developments like the flood of diving watches, GMTs, automatics and Hamilton electrics in the 1950s, but this isn't a detriment: you need to know how to boil an egg before you master a soufflé.

Wristwatches: A Handbook and Price Guide

Gisbert L Brunner and Christian Pfeiffer-Belli
ISBN 0-7643-2252-4. $19.95

Because of the wealth of knowledge that comprises the first section of this book, it's worth acquiring a copy – or the more recent 6th edition. It provides a concise history of the watch, how watches work, a glossary, how to collect and look after watches, how to avoid fakes and other topics that you should master as quickly as possible. While the prices are a waste of time, even for basic guidance as the values defy reality, everything else is solid: this prolific pair of German writers are the most capable watch authorities on the planet, seasoned veterans before certain self-appointed British 'experts' even hit puberty.

The World Of Watches

by Lucien F. Treub
ISBN 0-9706984-4-5. $85

First the good news: this is the finest volume I've ever found about watch brands, their histories and the way global watch manufacturing has evolved. Treub has written concise descriptions of just about every maker you can name, who's who in watches, a study of the technology, and more. It is simply the most-accessed reference book in my library. The bad news? Try finding a copy. I bought mine at the Baselworld watch fair, but even amazon.com returns screwy results – my latest search came up with a copy for $85, nearly double what I paid. But it's still worth every penny. Indispensible.

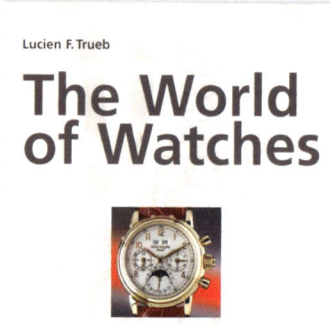

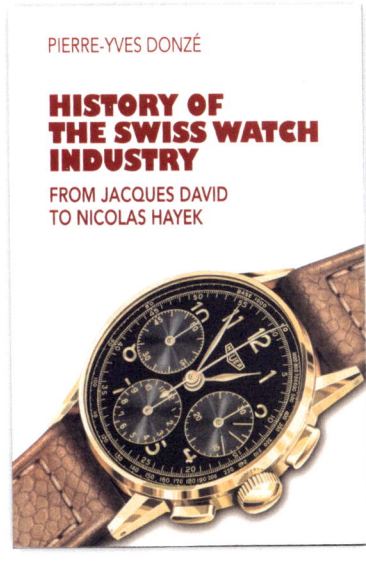

The History of the Swiss Watch Industry

by Pierre-Yves Donzé
ISBN 978-3-0343-1021-5. £35

It reads like a doctoral thesis, but then any book by a Swiss professor who teaches in Japan is bound to be academic. What this slim volume provides is a thorough study of the evolution of watch manufacturing, to provide you with an understanding of, for example, how the Americans lost it all to the Swiss, how the Swatch Group acquired so many brands and saved the Swiss industry, and much more, free of the kind of falsehoods perpetrated by the manufacturers, who have a penchant for 're-writing' history. It's dry, it's like being back at college, but you will leave it wiser than 95 per cent of the schmucks who write about watches for a living.

Dictionnaire Professionel Illustré de l'Horlogerie

by G.-A. Berner
Societé de Journal La Suisse
Horlogerie SA, Bienne, 2002. Circa

This fat volume is the definitive work on watch terminology. It's massive because it contains the 4790 definitions in French, English, Spanish and German. From the most basic terminology to the most obscure, this dictionary will save you the trouble of Googling terms like 'chablonnage', 'snail' and 'Breguet toothing', knowing that the definition is spot-on. Unlike the other books in this list, this is purely a reference work, and it is punitively expensive. You will have to surf the web to find a copy. But once it's clarified Dent's Anomaly for you, you'll wonder how you could live without it. Essential.

Numeral taken from the dial of a vintage pilots watch

THE INTERNET
PUBLISHER'S INTRODUCTION

In this chapter, I share my thoughts on how the internet has affected brands, consumers, product marketing and also impacted on production lines and volumes.

Two editorially eminent online experts join me: Robert Jan-Broer, - an expert in luxury brand online trends and owner of Fratello Watches - who discusses the internet as a whole, some brands that have taken advantage, and some interesting trend analysis; and Stephen J. Pulvirent, - former associate editor of Hodinkee and now luxury editor of Bloomberg – who gives us his views on how the consumer uses and communicates online.

THE INTERNET

IMPACT AND IMPORTANCE

Jacob Tomkins

The internet has allowed anyone in the world to become something of an expert. Where once one would need to scour encyclopedias, flick through dictionaries and consult directories and manuals to learn, we now are just a click and a tap away from research, facts and findings.

Pre-internet, being a fanatic on any specialist area was an entirely different hobby. Stamp collectors required a penchant for the dusty antique shop and dreary countryside brick-a-brack outlet; the crockery enthusiast had to have a keen eye and a compartmentalised map of where certain patterns or forms were kept, bought or sold. The mere act of being an enthusiast of something as specialised and hard to understand as watches, meant it was an absorbing, time consuming lifestyle in itself. The facts and relationships are so complex and interesting between materials and watchmakers, between brands and movements, between countries and horological techniques; but also to then know enough about all of it to make wise and informed buying decisions – this was a remarkable level of knowledge retained by dedicated fans.

These days, searching for a valuable purchase in the watch market is as simple as reaching into your pocket and pulling out your latest internet browsing gizmo. Having access to the right information does not necessarily mean, however, that people choose to use it, or even know how to find it.

The watchmaking industry has always held a lofty position in the luxury sector as one of the most high spend global markets, and as mentioned in earlier chapters, has been considered one of the most extraordinary mechanical feats of technological advance. The level of trade and fascination makes it potentially commercially rewarding if brands use it correctly.

In retail, the most important change is that the internet has opened the doors between consumers, and has allowed us to communicate with each other, as well as with the brands.

For retail brands in every sector, this has meant tighter competition both on price and quality, and sometimes lower margins. That may be a disadvantage in terms of standards, which might be lowered to protect margins, but it means that any good product has flourished with higher volumes and reach than before. The internet has allowed any watchmaker to become a brand with global presence. Watch buyers were already a well informed group, but whether buyers are fanatics or merely watch lovers, they do not make the decision to spend their several thousands lightly. A buyer is likely to have a carefully considered idea of what he or she wants to see on their own wrist, or sometimes an exact model in mind. There are very few impulse purchases. David Coleridge of The Watch Gallery told me that when they track their internet sales, there is an average of three months between the customer's first enquiry or viewing of the watch, and buying it.

1. We can buy from hundreds of sources online, and as online payment security and regulation has improved slowly but surely, it has become a safe environment in which to buy.

2. It also allows one to see aftermarket prices, helping the buyer better understand the long residual value of the watches. The extensive forums online can tell a buyer if a new product quality is low or high; if there are limited editions expected for release; if you should or should not buy in some cases, so how to be ahead of the curve.

3. All this extra information for the buyers on the aftermarket and long term value naturally pushes the buyer towards the more popular and more desirable brands, and particularly their most popular models (in turn these products and brands have bigger online marketing budgets to promote) Loyalty to brands has increased and therefore already collectible pieces become more so.

The internet has helped shape the market by mapping and monitoring strong trends in style and spend.

The main advantage of the information one can source online is that it is mostly independent. There still is heavy sponsorship and advertising controlling much of the content, but less than in the rest of the media and point of sale. The luxury watch brands love to control their marketing messages, which they are not able to achieve widely through the independent blogs and influencers online. They want complete control of their brand and product information, if possible. They also love to control their customer. The brands want to know who their customers are, and want to direct the purchasing process from the initial reading of their advertisement to payment at the store. They have struggled to do so more and more since the rise of the online forum.

Now that they do not have total control and we know more about production numbers, manufacturing processes, distribution, customer relations etc, a question commonly arises - what defines a luxury brand? Is it the experience of the brand? The exclusivity of the product? The style? The manufacturer's warranty? It certainly is a confusing subject, especially considering that most buyers for luxury products would say that the experience is not particularly pleasant, the products are produced in their millions and sometimes even the products themselves need explaining.

Shouldn't the brands be using the internet to promote the idea of luxury, to explain to us what is luxurious about their product other than its cost and materials?

Once upon a time, luxury meant exactly what it should. Highly limited production, exquisite personal attention and a rich experience for the customer. Nothing would be impossible in the world of true luxury, where price is no object. No longer. The internet has allowed the consumer to see the difference between something which is luxury, and something which is just a very clever and well marketed brand.

While all this is good news for the buyer, this does not always help the brand. Too much aftermarket activity can devalue the products – the only reason people buy from independent dealers and aftermarket trade houses is because of the price, and occasionally quicker delivery times. The Internet has changed the way people research and investigate investable purchases to make their buying decisions. It has enabled people to have direct contact with the brands and has also enabled the brands to speak directly to their consumers through an unregulated ever-changing platform. Previously luxury brands controlled all communication with the consumer through advertising, and the Internet has opened up new doors for people to be empowered by their abilities to access more information and better deals.

Linde Werdelin is a good example of a new brand to appear in the last fifteen years, which has taken advantage of the internet's ability to link them directly to consumers. It has enabled them to rapidly communicate many facts about their products or core messages which previously would have taken many more months through multiple channels of advertising. The internet has enabled a new marketing mindset for brands, allowing immediate and global communication, rather than waiting for print production, bill-board changes or TV advertising campaigns to take effect. Internet marketing can lead straight to the purchase.
The internet has systematically expanded every retail market and gradually made its way into the more controlled and regulated market segment of luxury brands. This access to information has empowered the consumer to be more critical and selective in their choices, forcing brands to improve levels of service and production.

DIRECT IMPACT
ON THE
INDUSTRY

Robert-Jan Broer

E-COMMERCE AND THE WATCH INDUSTRY – NOT QUITE THERE YET

Even in 2013, chances were high that you would get a notification on a brand's website that their watches cannot be bought through the internet. A bold statement. Does this mean that all watches you see for sale from this brand on the internet are not genuine products? According to Tudor for example, this seems to be the case. A short notification on their website tells you the following: "Genuine Tudor products are sold through Official Tudor Jewelers and are not available on the internet.".

However, other brands like Jaeger-LeCoultre, Panerai and Montblanc are selling watches or accessories directly through their websites in some countries. Smaller brands like NOMOS and Linde Werdelin have done so in an early stage as well and are quite successful with it in terms of sales.

THE ON-LINE WATCH COMMUNITY – THEY HELP GROW BRAND AWARENESS

In the case of Linde Werdelin you could say that this brand has gained a tremendous amount of attention due to the internet. The same goes for a number of smaller brands. Another example of such a brand is Sinn SpezialUhren from Frankfurt in Germany. You could categorise Sinn as an 'internet brand'. A brand that has gained world wide awareness due to the online community responsible for praising this manufacturer of functional and friendly priced watches.

Tudor is also a brand that has gained a lot from the online community. Their vintage watches are so popular amongst Rolex collectors that this is good reason for Tudor to recently come up with their Heritage line-up of watches. Ten years ago Tudor was a brand that was difficult to sell, in the USA it disappeared entirely from the market at one point. Since vintage Rolex timepieces have become so expensive due to the high demand for mint condition models, some of these collectors started picking up vintage Tudor Submariners and Big Block chronographs instead. These watches are a more affordable alternative for its bigger brother, Rolex. In 2013, Tudor decided to do a re-launch into the US market again.

LACKING GOOD STRATEGY AND POLICY MAKES OTHERS BENEFIT

While some big brands are still struggling to define a good strategy and policy for their internet presence and on-line sales, the on-line consumer for luxury watch brands benefits from the current offers on the internet already. The parallel market for watches – also being often referred to as a grey market – has almost a free play on the internet. Stock that comes from authorized dealers who need to make their turnover at the end of the year may disappear into the on-line shops of grey market dealers. 100% genuine watches, as opposed to what some luxury brands wants to make you believe, but not bought via the official retailer. Whether the consumer has voided their service warranty rights or not by buying outside authorised channels, the fact is that the consumer might be willing to take that risk with the discounts (sometimes up to 40% off retail) that are being given.

As long as an official dealer can explain their added value to the customer as opposed to buying on-line with a huge discount, the customer can make a well considered decision where to buy his or her timepiece. With the rapid increase of brand boutiques and official brand owned e-boutiques, the grey market of luxury watches will probably lose some of its market share to the authorised channels.

Above: Linde Werdelin Oktopus Moon Tattoo. Photo: Linde Werdelin
Opposite page: Sinn U1000-B Special Edition 2014. Photo: Sinn Spezialuhren GmbH

A GREAT MARKETING AND PR TOOL – TIME TO MEASURE

The internet is not about direct sales only; it is also a tool for marketers and PR departments to create awareness for their brands to a large public. By using social media such as Facebook, Twitter and Instagram, watch bloggers and forums as serious marketing channels, the brands realized they could reach a wider audience. An audience that prefers to read about their watches on-line instead of in good old books and magazines. Although it is difficult to measure the direct effect of these on-line marketing activities, the brand awareness can be measured and analysed and compared to the period before their on-line presence and activities..

That's another benefit from consumers going on-line to look out for a luxury watch. It creates the possibility to measure the consumer's interest and brand awareness, enabling the watch industry to get a better grip on the interest and demand for their watch brands and models. Perhaps the more the consumer uses the internet to trade, the more the quality of service and product will continue to increase.

This type of analysis can show some interesting figures. For some low production brands the demand is so much higher than for other brands with a much higher production volume. A good example here is Hublot. While the production number is estimated at approximately 25.000 watches (source Armband Uhren Katalog 2013, Heel Verlag), the demand for these watches is in some countries much higher than for watch brands that produce more than 10 times that number. Brands can benefit from this type of data to optimize their marketing activities and supply processes. Also, market data based on information from the internet can give insights into the preference of watch consumers for dial colors, type of complications, case materials or just about the most sought-after models. Although brands have this data based on their sales numbers, the internet enables them to have this data almost real-time and use it as predictive data (showing trends) as input for their R&D departments.

The top 10 luxury watch brands get approximately 60% of the share of searches by on-line watch enthusiasts. Even more amazing is the share that the number 1 brand (Rolex) gets, 21.78%. (measured by Chronolytics over Q2 2013)

Of course, when this analysis is being carried out in various price segments the share of online search traffic of brands will vary. A consumer that is looking for a 3000GBP timepiece is not the same as a high-end collector that is searching in the 20.000+GBP price segment. When the share of online search traffic is measured over all searches of watches in the >25.000GBP segment, the 1st spot is suddenly handed over to Patek Philippe with a 23.78% share.

This also shows that brands outside the top 10, or let us say outside the top 30, should be considered a real niche in the total volume of watches produced and offered for sale online.

Direct e-sales and allowing their retailer network to compete on the internet with the grey market will help brands benefit from the information it generates about their potential and existing customers, as well as the obvious advantage of more direct sales and customer relationships. The big brands have a lot of work to do here.

HOW
BRANDS AND CUSTOMERS USE
THE INTERNET

commentary. Stephen J. Pulvirent

In the early days, the watch industry was suspicious of the internet. And, to some degree, this was not entirely unwarranted. The first watch-centric sites to come to real prominence were mostly grey market retailers and people peddling fake watches, but eventually forums emerged along with independent publications, giving the disparate communities of watch enthusiasts places to gather and learn online. This has had a major impact on both the way watch buyers interact with brands and the way brands interact with potential buyers, as well as offering ways for watch collectors to come together and learn from one another.

Formerly, the best way for a customer to learn about a brand and to access the product was directly through the brand itself. Whether through advertising, visits to a boutique, or simply purchasing a watch, the customer was almost always placed in a sales environment if he or she wished to learn more. There were trade publications, but they were in many ways another extension of the industry itself. Online publications offered a non sales-driven venue where enthusiasts could learn from experts without the expectation of an immanent purchase. Immersive content such as in-depth interviews with important collectors and industry figures, beautiful videos, and large hands-on photographs of watches are all mainstays of what is done on blogs and open sites such as HODINKEE. This gives readers a way to experience what makes watch collecting so enjoyable from the perspective of people passionate about watches and telling the stories behind them.

Brands are beginning to realize in a big way that using these tools can help them tell their stories more vividly as well. Whether it's producing videos to offer three-dimensional looks at new releases or allowing brand representatives to participate in online forum discussions, watch brands are starting to utilize the tools of online media to give consumers an experience that feels more personal and substantial, something customers are coming to expect in the 21st century marketplace.

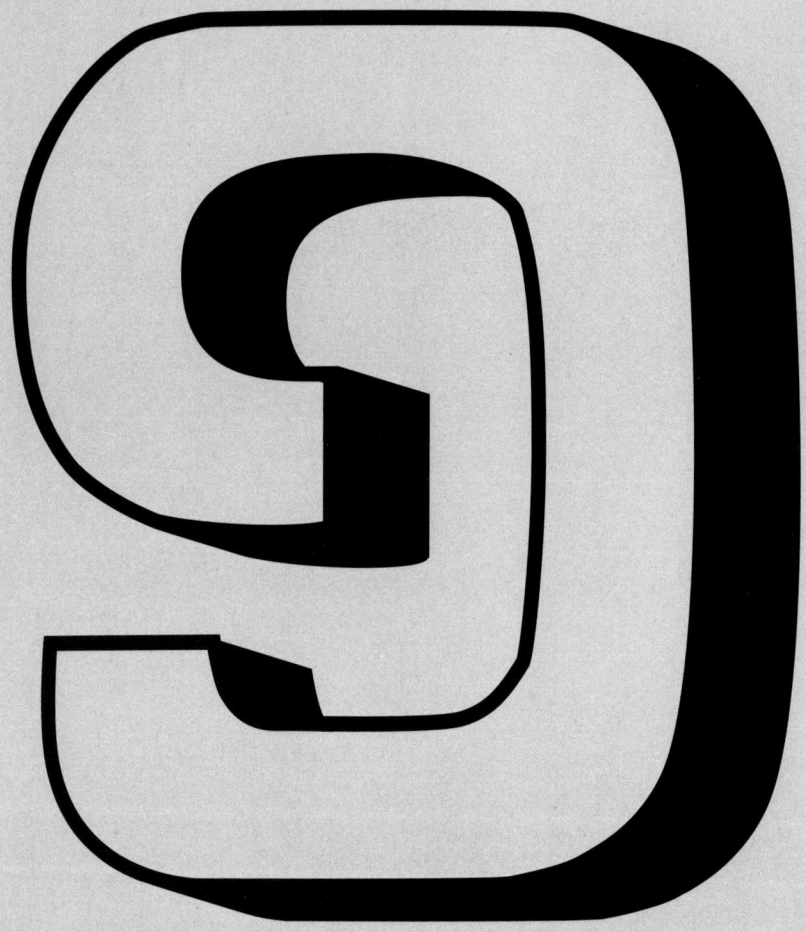

Numeral taken from a No name, Swiss made dial, 0s size 29.5. mm

WATCH AUCTION PRICE INDEX

Andrew Hildrith

WHY DO WE NEED A PRICE INDEX?

One of the questions facing the serious collector is: what is my watch collection worth now, and what will it be worth in the coming future?

If watches, as an asset, are a store of value, as well as something of value in terms of aesthetics and wants, then they will always have a price. The price is both a function of the intrinsic value from the manufacture of such pieces along with the demand (versus supply) of the watches in the market. The watch auction price index is a newly developed and unique way to monitor watch price movements based on open and fair transactions in the main auction markets. It tracks the current prices in international markets of a representative set of high quality watches and combines the price information into a monthly index to show, month by month, whether prices are going up or down, and by how much.

While there are always the 'headline' watches at any auction - the watches that support the belief that there are ever increasing prices for all serious watches - the index provides a way for the everyday collector and enthusiast to monitor the price of more typical quality watches they own or would like to own. For example, at the recent 'Lesson One' Christies Rolex Daytona auction, a Paul Newman Daytona went through the million US dollar price ceiling; an astounding price for a rare piece. However, while this watch caught the headlines, and collector attention, what about the more mortal investor who has a modest fraction of the record amount to spend? What will the potential return be on an investment of, say, $300,000 or $30,000? The index is designed to inform such collectors.

As it happens, Rolex 'Paul Newman' Daytona's (serial numbers: 6236, 6239, 6240, 6241, 6262, 6263, 6264) are the 'Blue Chip' investments of the watch world. One of the selected watches for the index, it has outperformed any other watch as part of the index. With an average year on year growth in Paul Newman Daytona's around the 11 percent mark for over a decade, even throughout the recent financial crisis, money on a good Rolex Paul Newman Daytona is often quoted as being a solid performing investment.

As conventionally secure financial instruments (supposedly relatively risk free) have not offered the same apparent predictability of performance returns over the past few years, capital has begun to seek out more diverse assets to hold. There has been a marked increase in funds that hold collectibles, rather than paper financial assets. But how to measure their performance over time?

Although there are some initial prospectuses and descriptions to be found in available public auction information, the watch index described here represents one of the first that measures the movement of real prices for watches in a meaningful and useful way. Compared to other collectibles, watches are a store of value, or a means to hold assets in much the same way as vintage cars, wine, or other 'object d'art' have been. With the growth in 'Collectibles Funds', where average annual returns are around the 5 percent mark, watches are one area that remains relatively unknown. Rumours abound about watch values, and watch prices seem to rise ever upward to the casual observer, but if the science of estimation is applied seriously to the auction prices of watches, then are watches really a store of wealth in the same category as other (semi-) liquid assets?

CONSTRUCTION OF THE PRICE INDEX

A price index, to be fairly representative of price movements in the market as a whole, needs to include the prices of commonly traded items and with transparent prices that reflect the prices an average private investor might face. Auctions have the distinct advantage over the brand watch boutique or authorised watch dealer in that an auction price can be deemed as the 'spot price' for a watch. It is a publicly available price established in an open auction which is a reflection of interested parties in the room. Wiling buyers and sellers at the auction establish the price on the day for the watch(es) as listed and potentially viewed. This means the condition of the watch and its specific features are known and the price reflects this. This is not the same with private sales and the auction index therefore does not include any private sales between collectors.

In this age of digital availability, both in terms of the items available at the auction and in the ability to bid (either on-line, by telephone, or by fax), the major auctions establish a global price for the item at that particular time. That said, there is nothing like 'being in the room' with the ability to handle and see the actual watch before the bidding begins. Hence, the index takes note of the location of the auction, and the currency in which bidding takes place. The ability to track prices over location and over time both allows for movements in foreign exchange and the ability to test if a global price for watches has become a realisation in recent years.

The purpose of the index is not to give the specific price of a watch at a given time; rather it is an indicator of the trend in price movements in the market for both vintage and contemporary watches. The watch index reports average price movements.

The watch index is currently composed of ten watches. The ten were chosen as representative of both long-run series watches, as well as more recent independent and established brands. The claim is not that the list is comprehensive and without the need for addition; rather it is a starting point based on well known and frequently traded watches that offer more reliable price indicators[1]. Obviously the long-run properties of the series are determined in large measure by the Patek and Rolex watches that have been in existence for a long time, either in terms of the auction market, or in terms of a continuous production run. The more recent watches are included into the index at the appropriate juncture; the construction of the index ensures that this does not cause an artificial 'jump' in the index.

While a result such as that witnessed at Christie's for the Rolex 'Paul Newman' Daytona may have a general effect on pulling prices upward, the normal sale of a 'one-off' watch will not. The index makes adjustment for condition and special features. In the case above, adjustments were made for the fact that the watch was in excellent condition, that it was part of a specialized auction solely for Rolex Daytona watches, and that the dial was nearly unique in terms of the font used for

---

[1] The index will be expanded over time by including other watches into the series as further reliable data becomes available.

'Daytona'. The price paid for that individual watch was high, and as established in public auction reflects the market's view of its unique value, but the price of such a 'one-off' watch would not distort the average real price of the auction index.

The index allows for, and incorporates, those features about a watch that make it unique. For example, if a watch had a unique dial, or metal case, inscriptions, or a change of movement. Likewise, the index takes note of the condition of the watch, and whether or not the watch was still supplied with case, papers, and the original guarantee. Allowing for all the relevant factors in the estimation, whether negative or positive, about the individual watch allows the index itself to track the path of average watch prices over time.

To construct the index to this point has required the recording of prices in watch auctions across the globe, the conversion of different prices into a single base currency (the US dollar) and to allow for differential inflation across nations. Even based on only 10 watches, the exercise has been data intensive. The prices that have been tracked came from the auction houses Bonham's, Christie's and Sotheby's, and Antiquorum.

The individual watch indices were spliced together weighted in one of two ways. The first method was by the number of watches of the same type sold that year as a proportion of the total number of watches believed to be manufactured. For a limited production series, that number was easily known. For others, it had to be estimated from what was known from reference books and estimates of total supply for the reference numbers concerned. Using these combined methods we are able to establish solid percentage averages in fluctuations and performance of those certain watches.

The watches selected for the index strike a balance between collectible watches, and some form of homogeneity in the watch itself. While the index does allow for differences in serial (model) numbers within type, the condition of the watch (as far as the grading scheme allows, which the trade will do so on a scale of 0-10, 10 being immaculate condition never worn, and 0 being un-repairable and relatively valueless), the case metal, the location and currency of sale, and any unusual recorded elements, there is still the issue of how far the index compares 'like with like' over time. Hence, as a way of incorporating some form of homogeneity across watches, the index includes a number of 'limited edition' watches that had appeared across the auctions over the last fourteen years. The inclusion of limited edition watches has the unique distinction that the watches are a known quantity in terms of supply, and that as the number of each watch is given as part of the auction catalogue, it would be possible in future to track the same watch over time as it appeared in different auctions [2].

For the one watch index where the same watch(es) did reappear at auction: the Patek 3940 'Officer' limited edition, the real price measured between the same watch was almost exactly the same as the real average annual growth for the watch type as given by the index. Although this is only one watch, it was reassuring to see that the estimation; allowing for different factors about the price and condition of the watch over timewas removing any individual factors about any individual watch, thus allowing the index to measure the prices over time.

---

[2] While the expectation had been that such measurement would be possible, and would therefore remove any particular features about the watches that were intrinsic to the watch, there was very little evidence of the same watches coming up for auction again, over time

WATCHES WHERE A 'BASE' CASE WAS NECESSARY WERE AS FOLLOWS:

ROLEX EXPLORER
Base model: New York, steel, reference 1016, good condition, US$, steel bracelet, no box/papers.

ROLEX "PAUL NEWMAN" DAYTONA
Base model: New York, steel, reference 6239, good condition, US$, steel bracelet, no box/papers.

PATEK PHILIPPE 2526
Base model: New York, cream dial, yellow gold, good, leather strap, no inscription, non-luminous markers, no box/papers.

PATEK PHILLIPE 5055
Base model: New York, yellow gold, good condition, US$, leather strap, no box/papers.

AUDEMARS PIGUET ROYAL OAK
New York, dark dial, steel, good condition, US$, steel bracelet, box/papers.
(N.B image shows the white dial version)

FP JOURNE RESONNANCE
New York, platinum case, yellow gold dial, good condition, US$, leather strap, box/papers.

GEORGE DANIELS MILLENIUM.
London, yellow gold, good condition, £Sterling, leather strap, box.

PATEK PHILLIPE OFFICERS' 3940.
New York, yellow gold, good condition, US$, leather strap, box/papers.

WATCHES WHERE THE SPECIAL EDITION HAD NO VARIATION IN THE CASE METAL OR MOVEMENT IN THE WATCH:

A. LANGE AND SOHNE ANNIVERSARY
New York, US$, box/papers.

JAEGER-LECOULTRE ROSE GOLD REVERSO TOURBILLON
New York, US$, box/papers.

ANALYSIS

The purpose of the index is not only to measure the real price growth in watches over the last 14 years (since 2000) but also to give a guide to what the future might hold for watch prices in the coming 5 years. As auction ('spot') prices are a daily quote - an auction on a particular day - the index was estimated on a day basis, but then averaged to an annual basis for presentation as an annual price index. As watches are rarely a short-term investment (the price does not vary greatly from one day to the next, or one month to the next), it makes more sense to analyse watch prices from one year to the next.

Figure 1 shows the graph for the overall index for average price levels (at the given date) for the whole time period. The watch index shows a number of interesting features. The first is that overall, the real watch price has increased by approximately 10 percent over the time period. What is interesting to note is that the index does reflect general movements in the real economy. Prices for watches dipped in 2002 – 03 and 2009 – 10. If collectors had the resources to acquire watches at auction during that time, then higher returns could have been achieved; as with other collectibles, timing is important. The large acceleration in the average annual real prices was from 2004 until 2008. Average annual real price growth was 2 percent a year during that time, whereas the index overall shows an approximate growth of 0.75 percent a year. There is some cyclicality within a year, as witnessed by the 'saw-tooth' pattern during the period.

Figure 1 also provides a different weighting to the individual watch series and gives an alternative view of the growth in auction prices. One factor that will definitely influence the price of a watch at auction would be the supply of watches to the auction market. Given a level of demand, if supply is more constrained one year than another, then this might be reflected in the price of the watches at auction. The weights that reflect supply were given as the number of watches (of a particular type) supplied to the market in a given year divided by the number of total watches available. Figure 1 shows that over the time period, the rate of growth in auction prices for watches was greater if supply considerations are included, and that the growth in auction prices was around 2004 and 2005 as demand outstripped the supply of collectable watches on the auction market.

Both indices from Figure 1 are also shown on Figure 2; however, the other index shown is for the average price of new Swiss mechanical watches. Once again, as with the auction price indices, the index for the average price of new mechanical watches accelerated for the first part of the decade, but continued to accelerate until 2008. Figure 2 illustrates that there was something of a 'bubble' in new mechanical watches that was not reflected in the auction prices for watches. Even now, recouping some of the price of a new watch purchased at peak prices in 2007 and 2008 would leave the collector at a loss. However, by 2010, the price of new mechanical watches had fallen in line with the auction price again and continues to do so until 2013 (when the current index ends).

FIGURE 1

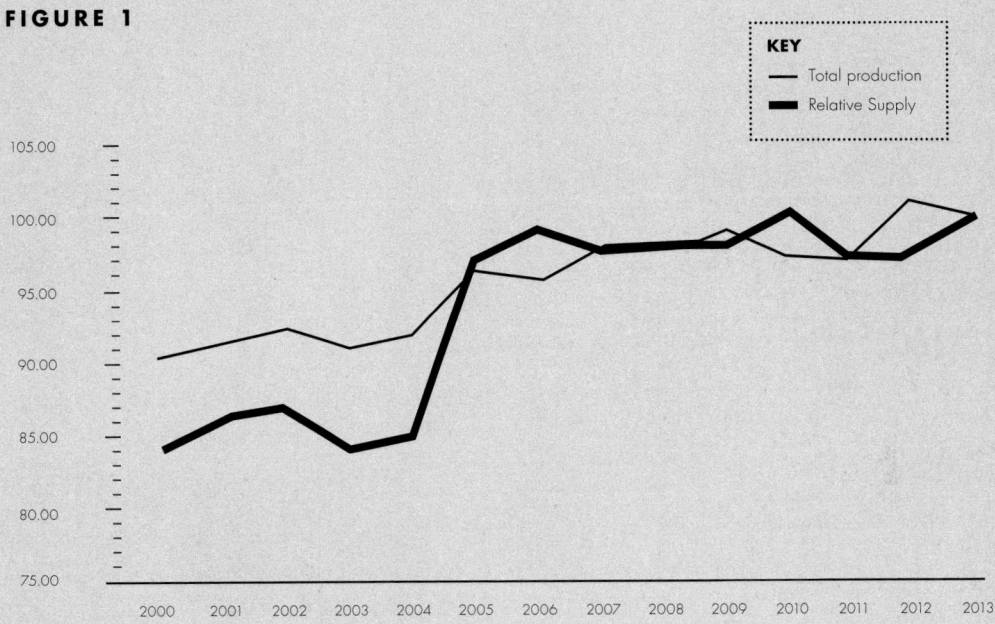

FIGURE 2

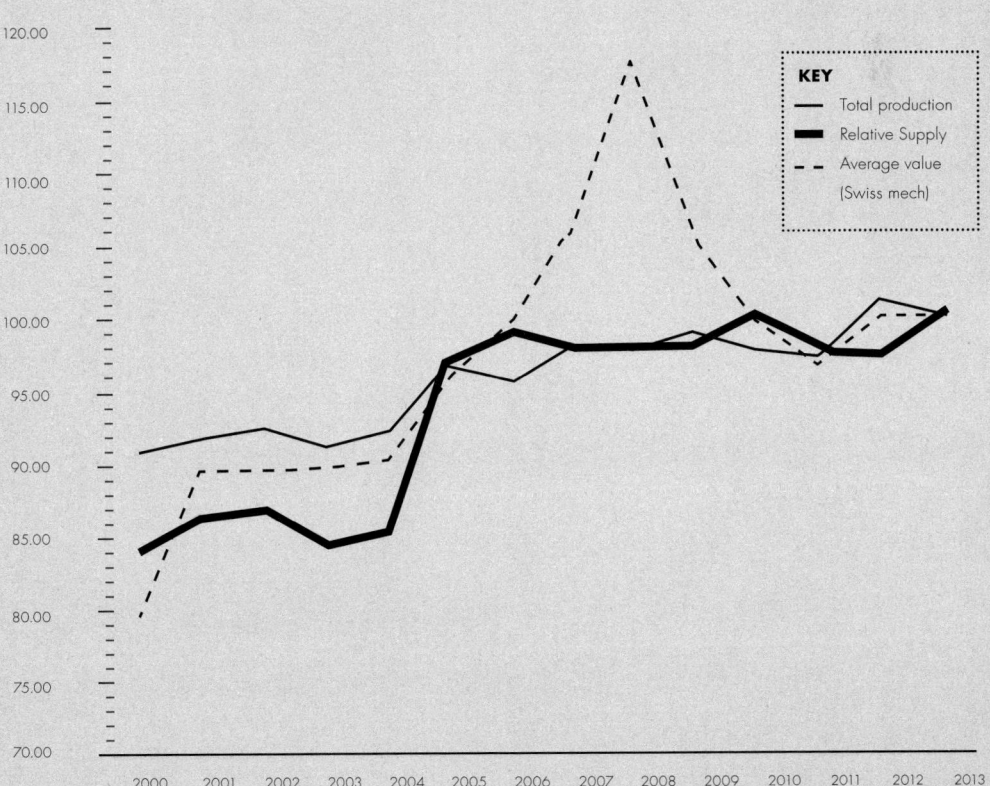

TABLE 1

ARITHMETIC AVERAGE RETURNS (PERCENTAGES) FOR INDIVIDUAL WATCHES	%
Rolex Explorer	3.98
Patek 2526	3.16
Rolex "Paul Newman" Daytona	10.47
Audemars Piguet Royal Oak	8.12
Patek Officers Anniversary 3940	2.51
Patek 5055	6.58
FP Journe Resonnance	1.31
Lange Sohne Anniversary	8.98
JLC Reverso Tourbillon	0.60
George Daniels Millenium	*

* Insufficient numbers sold to form an index for the time period

Table 1 provides the average annual price growth for each of the watches for the whole time period. The star of the show, for the past 14 years, has been the Rolex 'Paul Newman' Daytona. As witnessed by the 50 Year 'Lesson One' auction at Christies recently, 'Newman' Daytona's have managed to attain a near mythical status as a collection watch, and prices have grown as a result of that demand. The culmination of which was the recent dedicated Daytona event at Christies recently. The worst performing watch was the Jaeger-LeCoultre Reverso tourbillon. This was something of a surprise as the watch represents good value for money in terms of haute horologerie; in the eyes of collectors based on its price versus mechanical complexity and provenance. Also something of a surprise was the relatively low growth numbers shown by the Patek watches (especially the Patek 2526).

Another way of looking at the index would be to compare the return for any of the individual watches, or the portfolio of watches, against other relatively risk-free assets or indices. Table 2 compares the average annual returns for three US based assets: the S&P500, the 3-month Treasury Bills (seen as risk free short-term assets), and 10-year Treasury Bills (seen as long-term risk free assets).

What is remarkable is that the return on the portfolio of watches would perform in line with any of the other assets. In particular, it is worth noting that the watches would not only provide an asset that can be enjoyed (in being worn or admired), but should the portfolio be revised longer term, the returns are equivalent to other comparable long-term and low risk assets.

TABLE 2

ARITHMETIC AVERAGE RETURNS (PERCENTAGES)	%
Watch index - US$ - overall average annual (2000-2013)	5.69
S&P 500*	8.71
Three-month US Treasury Bill*	1.65
Ten-year US Treasury Bill*	5.64

* Figures from:
http://pages.stern.nyu.edu/~%20adamodar/New_Home_Page/datafile/histretSP.html

The arithmetic averages were calculated for 2002 - 2012 (inclusive).

TABLE 3

ARITHMETIC AVERAGE RETURNS 2000 - 2013 (PERCENTAGES)	%
Predicted index (2011 - 2013)	5.37
95% Lower Confidence (2011 - 2013)	2.56
95% Upper Confidence (2011 - 2013)	10.90

While the index performs well against other financial assets, there is also the question of how stable is the index over time. In other words, how well does the index perform in predicting future prices or price movements? To assess how well the index predicts future prices, a 'within-sample' prediction was assessed to examine how accurately the index could predict prices 3 years into the future. Around any prediction (which itself is an estimate) is a confidence interval (degree of uncertainty) that was assessed at a 95 percent level of confidence.

The results of the prediction are given in Figure 3 and Table 3. Figure 3 shows that the index predicts accurately: the predicted index almost lying on top of the actual index for the 3 years. However, the 95 percent confidence interval shows that in years of high price volatility (such as 2012), where the price for a particular watch was not consistent across geography or across auctions, the growth in average auction prices could be considerably greater or lower. Table 3 gives the average annual growth in real prices at auction where the last 3 years were either the predicted index, the

95 percent lower confidence level, and the 95 percent upper confidence level. The predicted index, where the last three years were predicted (2011 – 2013), has a slightly lower average annual growth in real prices, but the difference is negligible. At the 95 percent confidence interval, in other words, if we could hypothetically run the same (experiment) sample of observations an infinite number of times, then it is possible that the average annual growth could be as low as 2.5 percent, or as high 10.9 percent. The variability comes from two sources. The first is that the index is only estimated off ten watches. Although arguably representative of a collectors' portfolio, it is nonetheless a limited set. The second source of variability lies in the year to year variation in prices of the watches, and the heterogeneity of the watches themselves. In future editions of the index, the addition of more watches to the series, and the addition of data to the index, will see better definition in the predictions and the degree of certainty in the index.

FIGURE 3

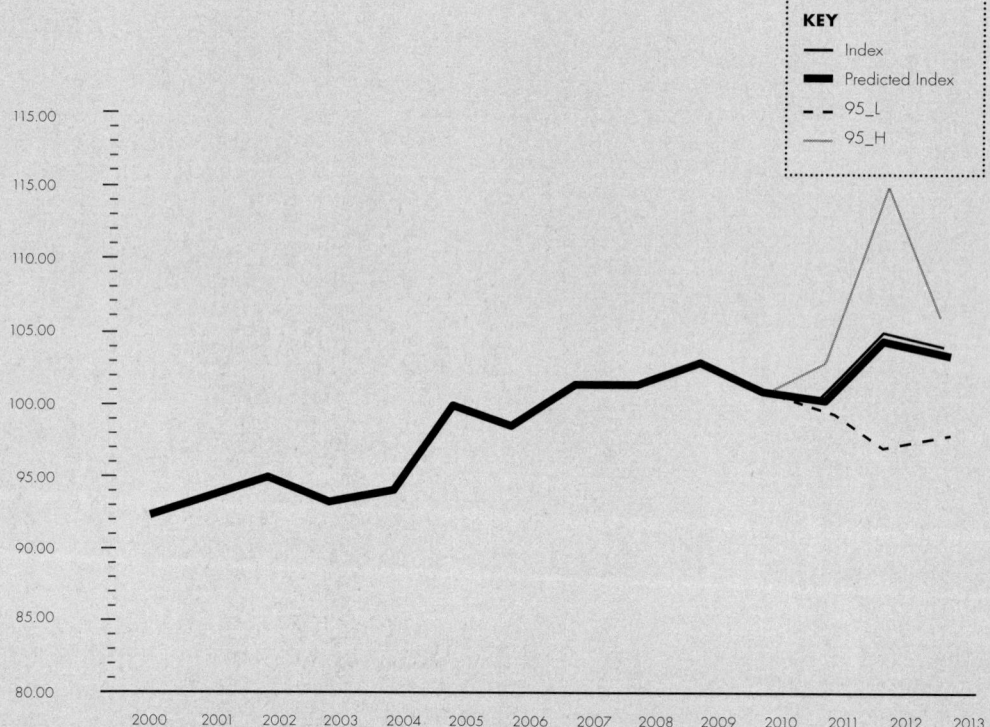

POTENTIAL VALUE OF A USD 10,000 WATCH BOUGHT IN 2000– YEAR ON YEAR
(BASED ON THE INDEX GIVEN)

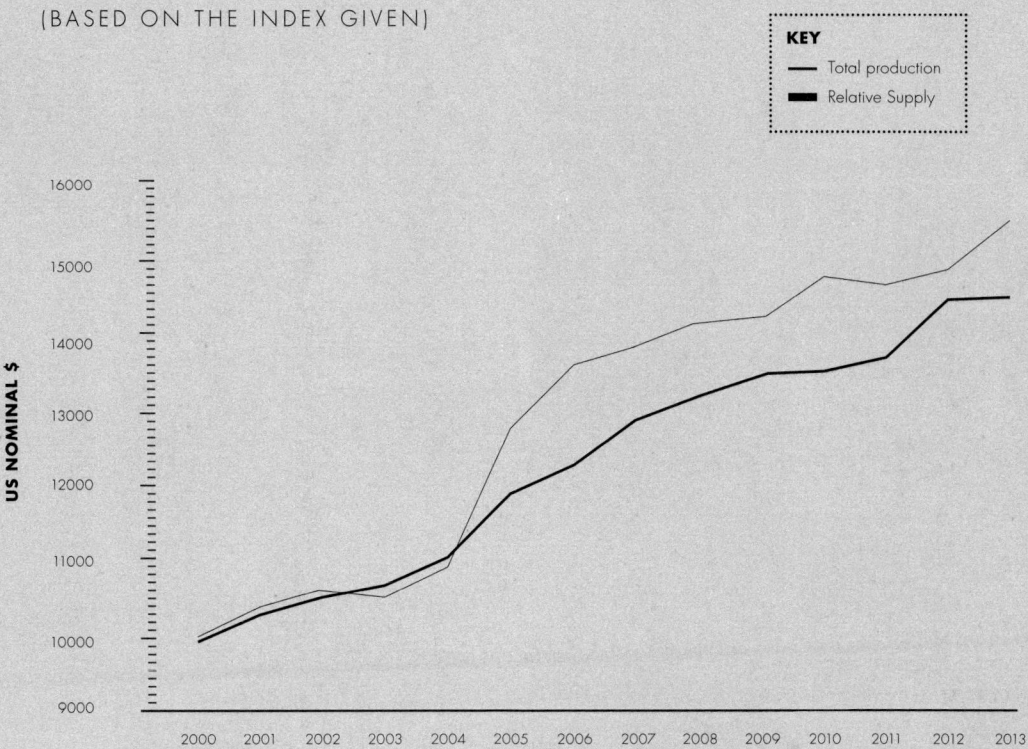

DATE	TOTAL PRODUCTION	RELATIVE SUPPLY
01/01/2013	14472.6108239554	15499.6998461203
01/01/2012	14435.0567847529	14902.2957072521
01/01/2011	13650.8198699042	14719.584406966
01/01/2010	13400.7391950302	14785.0207318025
01/01/2009	13397.3947173517	14218.8523017753
01/01/2008	13259.8653174948	14192.9391892434
01/01/2007	12930.3342188456	13791.6175121696
01/01/2006	12262.369167238	13623.1445767753
01/01/2005	11973.8052962462	12884.1964461199
01/01/2004	11041.2812907506	10946.5347917782
01/01/2003	10641.4102248809	10531.0151819746
01/01/2002	10557.6119304722	10614.7724676545
01/01/2001	10324.0672606058	10417.498165518
01/01/2000	10000	10000

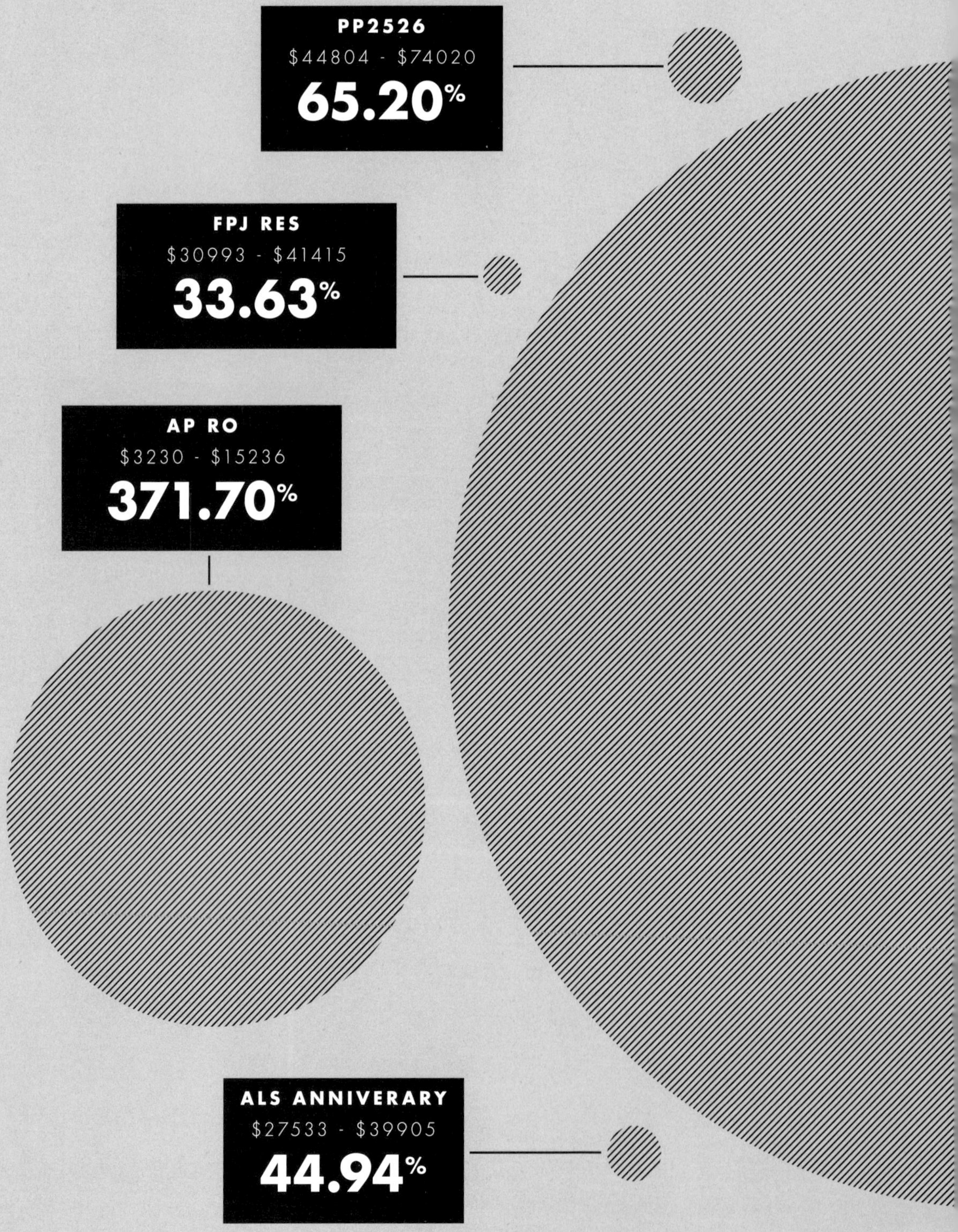

PP2526
$44804 - $74020
65.20%

FPJ RES
$30993 - $41415
33.63%

AP RO
$3230 - $15236
371.70%

ALS ANNIVERARY
$27533 - $39905
44.94%

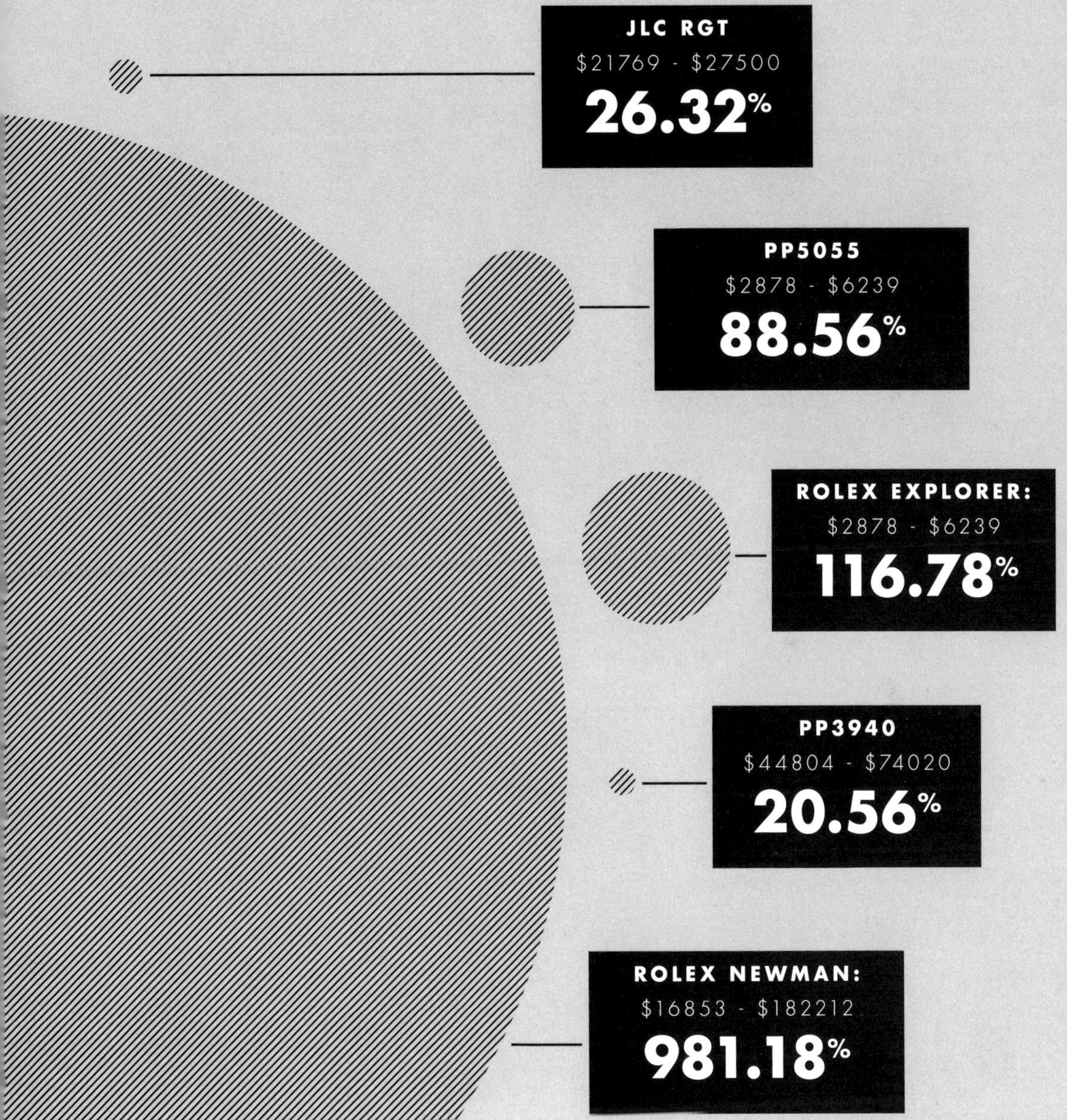

JLC RGT
$21769 - $27500
26.32%

PP5055
$2878 - $6239
88.56%

ROLEX EXPLORER:
$2878 - $6239
116.78%

PP3940
$44804 - $74020
20.56%

ROLEX NEWMAN:
$16853 - $182212
981.18%

Note that these average figures are JUST the average prices paid for watches within each category within that year.

As such, these figures are a broad and approximate range only. There is no allowance specifically for different watch characteristics.

Numeral a re-drawing from original artist sketches of a typeface developed specifically for IWC Da Vinci line.

BRANDS AND MILESTONES
PUBLISHER'S INTRODUCTION

At certain intervals, and from different corners of the industry, we have seen some watchmakers and brands entirely change the face of time keeping and watch making. Throughout this journal we refers to and discuss many important and relevant brands and watches., However, this chapter specifically highlights a few select individual brands, watchmakers and designers that we feel are really worth exploring in detail.

These are brands which have clearly changed the landscape of the industry. We will cover new individual companies and watchmakers in each issue, but to start, we cover three. What makes these three interesting to contrast and important in nature are that without compromising the core values of their work, and without limits to what is considered possible, each has pursued and succeeded in doing things no other watch makers achieved. In doing so, they have contributed to this already phenomenal art.

The three covered here are George Daniels, Richard Mille and Jaeger-leCoultre. 2013 celebrated the 180th anniversary of Jaeger le Coultre – not part of the 'holy trinity' of watch brands Vacheron Constantin, Patek Philippe and Breguet, but certainly can be known as one of the heritage brands, and one of the most collectible. 2011 saw the sad loss of one of the greatest minds in horology – George Daniels – who will always be remembered for his exceptional, traditionally hand made pieces and his contribution to general time keeping with the Co-axial movement calibre. Thirdly, a newer and more controversial brand - Richard Mille – who is breaking the mould on watch ergonomics, case material use and production, expanding on imagination with his full sapphire crystal cases and lightweight designs.

Andrew Hildreth shows his in depth knowledge and love for all three of these focus brands, highlights some details of their achievements and why we feel they should be recognized as industry icons.

GEORGE DANIELS:
THE WATCHMAKERS WATCHMAKER

Andrew Hildreth

GEORGE DANIELS CBE, DSC, FBHI, FSA

They are often over-used terms: 'genius', 'greatest', 'without equal', but all are often applied to George Daniels in terms of watchmaking, and in this instance, with good reason. Whatever individuals might think of his work, generally there is a consensus that George was the independent watchmakers' independent watchmaker. Throughout the worst years of the mechanical watchmaking industry in the past three centuries, not only did he show others that survival was possible, but perhaps more importantly that the mechanical watch could hold advantages over the electronic counterpart; that a mechanical watch, over the long run, could both be more accurate and run without human intervention; that the mechanical watch, designed, manufactured, and finished to the required standards, would not only be an accurate timekeeping mechanism, but also a store of value because of the handwork and craftsmanship it contained.

George died in late 2011 knowing that his work was secure, his place in the pantheon of horological greats unquestioned, and the effects of his invention would continue in the watches made and produced by others. George's life was all in good time and well spent!

His life story is the classic one of 'rags to riches'. Born in Edgware, London in 1926, one of eleven children, he had a difficult upbringing. There are claims he was illegitimate, that his father (a carpenter) was a drunk, and that the family perpetually struggled for money. George's life changed when he was five; he became fascinated by watches when he found a cheap wristwatch in the street. Upon opening it, George became mesmerized by the mechanism; for George, the watch contained the whole universe. From then, he knew what he wanted to do with his life.

George Daniels went to work at the age of fourteen and was then conscripted into the Army. He taught himself the repairing of watches and clocks. Back in England, George started work with a watchmaker in Edgware, attending evening classes in horology at Northampton Polytechnic which eventually merged into the site of City University, London. Initially he repaired watches in order to finance his love of vintage cars. A chance meeting in 1960 with Sam Clutton, a founder member of the Antiquarian Horological Society and the Vintage Sports Car Club in Britain, introduced him to upmarket and antique horology. Clutton introduced him to the work of Breguet. Daniels became such an expert on the French horologist that he subsequently restored many Breguet watches, and in 1967 was invited to take over the Breguet company. He declined the offer reasoning that: 'Daniels, London' sounded better to him than: 'Breguet, Paris'.

By 1969 Daniels had produced his first mechanical watch. He sold the piece to Clutton, who showed it to other collectors, and Daniels embarked on his career as a specialist watchmaker. Daniels had three rules in starting to produce his own watches. The first was that he was not going to make watches to order. A watch would have to be to George's own design, have a purpose in terms of horological research, and be completed to George's satisfaction. He refused to take orders and the watch would only then be sold providing George could find someone suitable. Daniels was particular about his customers: "I was very selective," he recalled. "I never made watches for people if I didn't care for them." Second, the appearance of the case, dial and movement should make it instantly recognizable as a Daniels watch. Third, to make sure that the watch included mechanical features that would appeal to the collector. To be a Daniels watch, the watch must have "… historic, intellectual, technical, aesthetic, amusing, and useful qualities."

Consequently, there are only 37 individual watches that George created outside of his Millennium and recent Anniversary series, both the latter series produced in collaboration with Roger Smith. As such, each of the 37 watches is considered a work of art in their own right, coming up for auction infrequently. At the Sotheby's November 2012 auction, for the George Daniels Trust (liquidating George's work and possessions), George's generally acknowledged masterpiece, the Space Traveler watch, realized a galactic £1.15 million (not including buyer premium or VAT). This is somewhat fitting for a watch that would record the time beyond the stratosphere and that could help you tell time "… on your package tour to Mars … " (as George argued). Considering that the first pocket watch was sold to Clutton for £5000, George Daniels' watches have shown considerable return.

Even the Daniels Millennium watches, when they come up for auction, have increased in price steadily since George sold them to people that he liked. Depending on the gold metal in the case, the price ranges from over £100,000 (for the rarer white gold version) to about £80000 (for the more traditional yellow gold version). There are rumours that the price for a new Millennium watch varied by George's estimation of how much you could pay, and the degree to which he liked you! George's lasting contribution to horology was through his co-axial escapement. This was largely ignored or rejected by the Swiss watch industry until Omega, as part of the Swatch Group, decided to fit the escapement to all of their high end watches from 2000. George always had a number of stories about how each time a concern was raised about the ability to fit the co-axial into the movement, George would show the Swiss concern in question how it could be done. At the Worshipful Company of Clockmakers Museum at the Guildhall in London, there is a Patek movement fitted with a co-axial escapement. At the Sotheby's Auction in November 2012 (for the George Daniels Trust), there was the chance to buy a Rolex, an Urban Jurgensen, and a Hamilton (with an ETA movement) all fitted with a co-axial escapement. All watches are working and keeping time without any problems. In one of our final conversations he told me that: "I had to do it; I had to make sure that the development I had laboured for, for so long, was not consigned

George Daniels Millenium (back)
Photo: Andrew Hildreth

to the footnote of history. I sold it at a loss; the development of the co-axial had cost me more than I made on it."

Talking to George a few months before his death (in 2011), I enquired as to whether Omega had reported any longer term savings in terms of maintenance on the coaxial watches. George had no idea. On some of the pocket watch movements, where the co-axial had been fitted, the fourth wheel had some small metallic deposits building up (visible through a high powered microscope), but no one could fathom out why. Only time will tell whether George's co-axial really did deliver longer run accuracy with less maintenance.

George did it all! He invented the life he wanted to live: watches to his own design; owning and racing vintage cars, and making his mark in both spheres: the coaxial for watches; restoring Sir Henry 'Tim' Birkin's racing machines for vintage cars. Thankfully George never did forget which hammer should be used where.
George Daniels was Master of the Worshipful Company of Clockmakers, awardedthe Gold (Tompion) Medal of the Worshipful Company of Clockmakers; the Gold Medal of the British Horological Institute; the Gold Medal of the City of London; and the Kullberg Medal of the Stockholm Watchmakers' Guild. He was granted an honorary doctorate from his alma mater City University, who are now, incidentally, one of the primary beneficiaries of the George Daniels Trust.

George showed other independent watchmakers how to not only survive, but how to cultivate their own style and body of work. How to be sure of using their own name, rather than feel they should borrow another 'brand' name. A couple of years before his death, F.P. Journe not only gifted a platinum version of his Chronometre Souverain, he inscribed it 'FP to George Daniels my mentor.' The expansion of independent watchmakers, and the reverence with which artisan watchmaking is held, is due in large part to the path blazed by George Daniels. Unlike current independent watchmakers, who are inclined to production runs on watches in
triple figures, George's watches are still a rarity. With so very few George Daniels watches in existence, one thing is for sure: the price of such rarities will continue to rise. And that's if the lucky few who currently own them will want to part with one of their prized possessions.

RICHARD MILLE:
CASE REVOLUTIONS

Andrew Hildreth

In a little over a decade Richard Mille has gone from a watch company with a single design, to one of the most sought after watches in the luxury market. In fact, testimony to that are the recent rumours of a takeover by PPR that will in all likelihood be borne out in the early months of 2014. That Richard succeeded in building a brand image with principally one design for a watch case is equally testimony to the design itself and how Richard adapted the design to suit new materials. If there has been one watch brand that has pursued exotic new case material and new movement design in the past decade, then it is Richard Mille.

Value for Richard Mille stems from the intrinsic workmanship embodied in the watch and not necessarily because of the use of precious metals or stones. As the man himself is often fond of pointing out, the actual cost of the precious metal for case manufacture is small compared to the cost of the number of man and machine hours in honing down a hunk of material (metal or some other substance) to a polished and finished article. For Richard, the value of an object is in the emotion and desire it evokes, and that comes from technique and finishing, and not because of its weight in gold!

While Richard's watches often use exotic or esoteric material in case or plate construction, the actual movement components are made from traditional metals and finished to the highest standard. There are exceptions from this rule: the RM018 had gear wheels that were made from semi-precious stones; movements have carbon nanofibre or titanium back or main plates. But while some watch firms have experimented with silicon gear wheels, or a silicon hairspring, Richard Mille watches have retained movement parts that would grace any traditionally designed and finished watch. Where Richard Mille watches differ markedly from others is in the design and the techniques involved in the use of new case material; and how he differentiates his watches from others in the market.

The original watch case design itself came from Richard's own love of technique. While there is a simple beguiling curve to the outside, the Richard Mille case shape is more complex than it first appears for a number of reasons. A great deal is made of other cases, from other watch firms, but the complexity of the Richard Mille case is in the required exactness and finish for three separately machined parts to function as a completed whole.

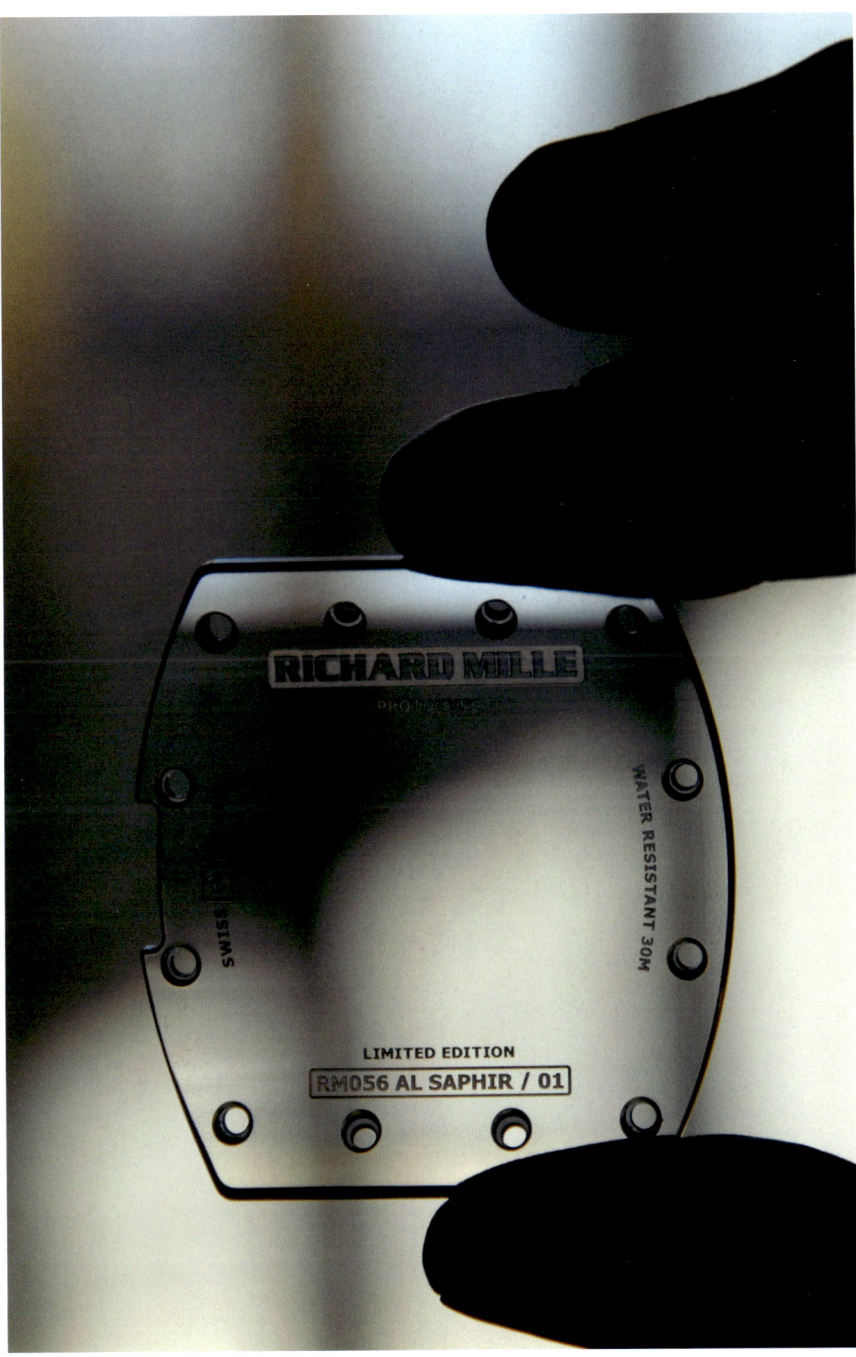

Richard Mille 'Tonneau' case shape - caseback from the RM056/01
Photo: Andrew Hildreth

Top: RIchard Mille RM056-01, case entirely made from sapphire crystal.
Bottom: Richard Mille RM017 Tourbillon Titanium - back.
Photos: Andrew Hildreth

The Richard Mille tonneau curved case shape represents one of the more complex to be found in the watch making industry. The degree of complexity in what appears to be a simple shape is beguiling and the case is definitely a 21st Century design, inception and execution. From the beginning, perhaps more than any other element, the shape and design of the case has defined the look of the Richard Mille watch and made it instantly recognizable. In only a decade, from the advent of the tonneau shaped case first seen with the RM001, the Richard Mille case has become a design icon.

Completed in three elements the case is tactile and form fitting on seemingly any wrist. The case is a reflection of Richard Mille's love of technique in the car racing and aviation fields. In an early interview (about six months after Richard Mille S.A. had started, Richard described his watch case as:
"The case has a strong personality as I wanted to create a very different object, extremely ergonomic with characteristic lateral ribs of improved rigidity, a large size and easy-to-grip hand setting crown, easy to read watch with clear numbers and anti-glare treatment on sapphire glass. In total, an efficient, relentless watch, no gimmick, no glamour. It is a global and integral approach to the movement, case, dial. This means everything has been designed by starting from a clean sheet, according to an extremely precise and rigorous specification, with the aim of completely integrating all the elements, like a Formula 1 car where the chassis and the engine are both developed together. " – see http://www.thepurists.com/watch/features/interviews/MilleApr02/index.htm.

Creating the complex cases was originally entrusted to one of Switzerland's top case makers: Donzé Baume. However, since Donzé Baume was acquired by the Richemont Group, Richard has invested considerable resources in building his own case manufacture. The front bezel, the caseband (holding the movement and crown), and the back bezel: all three have to be manufactured to fit perfectly together so that when bolted into a single form there is not a sliver of space in between each part to let in either dust or moisture to damage the movement. The tolerances are tested to ensure exactness as any case shape away from the round example (such as the tonneau) presents problems as the forces acting on the case (in depth rating) are not uniform throughout.

There is a long series of technical steps that will take you from Richard Mille's original drawing to the finished technical drawings and CAD programs that will manufacture the case. Every part of the Richard Mille case is designed to the most precise detail. Richard Mille cases have become an art form in their own right over the past decade. As watch manufacturers have generally tried using different materials, it is Richard Mille that both pioneered the modern/material science approach to watchmaking, and has continued to push the boundaries on what is possible. In terms of pricing his watches, collectors have wondered why the new material watch is so expensive when compared to a gold case watch. Some pricing economics will hopefully clear this up. The basic blank of titanium (or whatever material is being used) is usually less expensive than the equivalent in gold or platinum, but the difference becomes minimal when the costs of machining and finishing the complex case are included.

The case starts to take shape through a number of stages at CNC (Computer Numeric Cutting) machines. It is an exacting form of art, but one small mistake and the case is sent back to the foundry to start life again in the form of a new blank. Inside the CNC machine the blank is consumed in a deluge of oil and cutting tools.

Little by little, in several stages using several different machines, then reduced down until the finished piece finally evolves from the metal. Once out of the CNC machine, the case still has to be finished by hand, again in several stages and by different people, removing burrs, cleaning and polishing rough edges, and visually checking all parts for cleanliness of execution.

Once the case is in recognizable form, it is then further hand finished and polished along all edges, and all surfaces, to ensure that the case will fit perfectly and there are no loose edges. The case is then subjected to further testing, finishing, and fitting the crystals as required. To ensure that the case has been made to the required exacting standards, the cases are then subjected to further testing using laser reference points. On a piece of perfectly flat milled marble the case parts are individually tested. The laser then reads 'points' over the curved surface of the case parts. Measurement is to a 100th of a millimeter and is undertaken to ensure that the 3 elements of the case will fit together perfectly. The smallest of gaps between any of the case elements will compromise the seal (as there is no ring seal in the Richard Mille case) and the case will be rejected in water resistance testing.

Given that all elements of the case pass measurement, and the dimensions are assured, the next stage is to finish the metal surfaces by polishing. The polishing is an art form in itself. The Richard Mille case is particularly complex because of the form of the case (especially in the caseband section with the vertical ribs). There have been variations on this design with watches such as the RM014 having polished lateral ribs on a brushed background. Such exacting finish is something that distinguishes the Richard Mille case. Because of the way the case is designed, the watchmaker has only to 'bolt' the movement to the case (mid-section), as well as mount the necessary bezel rings and crystals for the watch to be complete.

In the years since the use of gold and platinum, and a case in titanium (one of the first on the market), Richard has produced cases/plates in a range of materials some of which seem the stuff of science fiction. It is at this nexus point where material science meets horology that Richard Mille is at his best. The materials used in the watches have ranged from ALUSIC (Aluminum AS7G Silicium Carbide – AlSiC): a material that requires centrifugal casting and labourious milling operations. So much so that initially the milling of the RM009 ALUSIC cases burned through the machining bits leaving the ingots unblemished! New techniques were required to machine the RM009 case. Other materials for case or plate parts have comprised carbon nanofibre (RM006), orthorhombic titanium aluminide (orthorhombic TiAl (OTiAl) honeycomb core) for the RM021, polymer composite with carbon nanotubes (RM027), magnesium aluminum AZ91coated in crystalline oxide ceramic (MgAl2O4) spinels (RM038), silicon nitride (RM011), and more recently sapphire crystal (RM056).

To undertake the case for the RM056 Richard turned to Switzerland's (and possibly the worlds) foremost crystal firm: Stettler Sapphire. Stettler produce the sapphire crystals for a number of high end watch firms; certainly a few from the Richemont Group, from the LVMH group, and other larger and smaller independents who require complex crystal shapes for their watches (for example, the MB&F HM4). Richard uses Stettler for the crystal dials on his watches so he knew of their capabilities in the market and the quality of their sapphire crystal. Most of us wear a watch with a Stettler sapphire crystal covering the dial.

A crystal is a solid material whose constituent atoms, molecules, or ions are arranged in an orderly repeating pattern extending in all three spatial dimensions. Similar to a diamond, it makes sapphire crystal second only to diamond in terms of hardness.

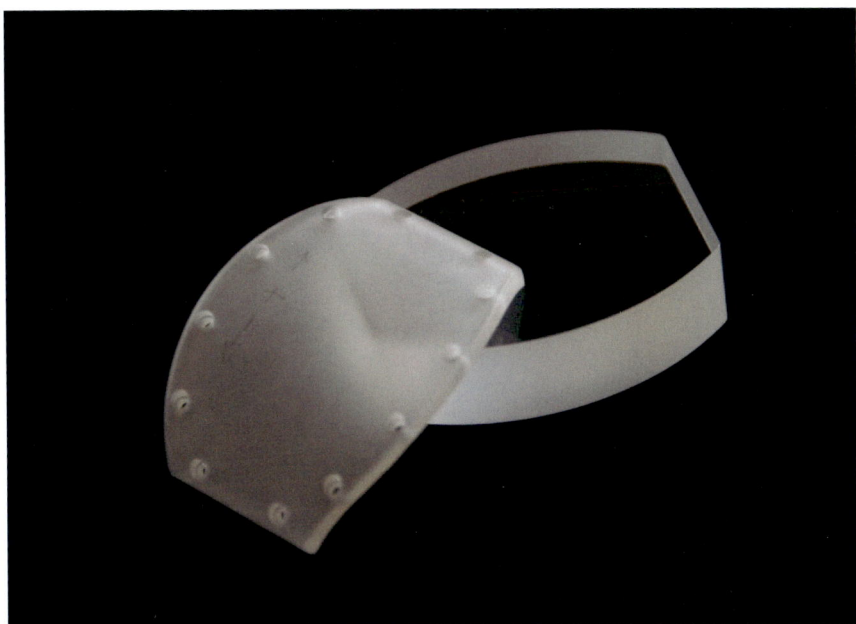

Top: Richard Mille 'Tonneau' case shape - before/after caseback sapphire from the RM056/01
Bottom: Richard Mille 'Tonneau' case shape - main sapphire body (unpolished) from the RM056/01
Photos: Andrew Hildreth

It makes the crystal resistant to any changes in shape, but by the same token, it is very difficult to machine into a complex shape. Crystals are grown from an initial seed by a variety of methods. The resulting raw crystal shapes are then used for a number of different purposes. Crystals for more complex shapes are grown by the Kyropoulos method which allows the growth of large sapphire crystals with a first or second grade optical quality. It is crystal grown by this method that is used in the Richard Mille RM056 case.

Other watch brands have attempted crystal watch cases, but generally, the case has been round, with flat surfaces, and without any complexity inside the case that is required to hold the movement. What is different about the Richard Mille RM056 watch case is the three part structure, where the three parts have to fit to within a required accuracy down to the 1/100th of a millimetre. The watch case has to be a fully functioning Richard Mille case with a water resistant rating of 30 metres. It is one of the most complex case shapes to manufacture, even when the case is made out of known materials. The upper and lower parts of the case are both curved and non-monotonic. In other words, the curvature is not a constant over the surface: shallow at one part, slightly steeper in another. With an exact CNC machine, such curved surfaces can be achieved within the necessary tolerances.

For sapphire crystal, such cutting and polishing is a whole new problem. Chief among the new set of problems to overcome is that while you can cut the general shapes for the crystal parts for the case, it is the finishing and polishing where the problems really start. The real problem is that the polishing cannot be seen! Submerged within a pot of viscous sand, the polishing takes place in an area where no measurement can be taken. To polish the surfaces to the standard required, the piece has to be removed from the polishing machine and periodic measurements made. Anything not within the 1/100th of a millimetre tolerance (at all points of contact between the case parts) the part is rejected and the process starts all over again.

Further problems arise with the drilling of the holes for the screws, pushers and crown. At any one moment the drilling can cause the crystal to crack or shatter and all the work thus far is lost. The whole process seems to just be waiting for a disaster to happen! The middle part of the Richard Mille case is intricate and contains a number of ridges where the movement is screwed into the case. All ridges and surfaces had to be polished to an exacting standard. There is nowhere to hide in a crystal clear case!

To give the 'cost' of the RM056 case some metrics, to gauge the scale of the problem, consider the following. One way to gauge the cost of the RM056 case is to consider what else could have been achieved with the same resources (an opportunity cost). Think of it this way, instead of producing the five Richard Mille RM056 cases (the complete run for the special edition), Stettler could have produced approximately 60000 curved watch crystals in the year. The annual production for the whole factory would be about 120000. In other words, producing the RM056 cases represents half of Stettler's annual production. The five RM056 cases will take a year to produce; or about 2 and half months each.

The work also required considerable investment by Stettler (underwritten by Richard's order). Without the advent of the new ultrasound polishing and cutting machines, all of which had to be acquired for the new work, the project would not have been possible. As with any other material Richard uses in his watches, the RM056 sapphire crystal case is at the outer limit of what is known and possible.

THE WATCHMAKER'S WATCHMAKER:
JAEGER-LECOULTRE AT 180

Andrew Hildreth

With Jaeger-LeCoultre celebrating 180 years since foundation in 2013, and with another tour de force set of watches launched as part of that celebration, it is worthwhile taking a look back and recording how Jaeger-LeCoultre gained their reputation. Their reputation is second to none; they have been until recently the Swiss watchmakers' watchmaker. Untold numbers of base ebauche left Jaeger-LeCoultre from the 1930's up until just recently. And it is worth noting that should your vintage Cartier or Vacheron need new parts, it would probably be worthwhile contacting Jacger as most of the machine tool bits for manufacturing the parts can be found in the same factory as whence they came from in Le Sentier.

It is only recently, in the last decade, as other watchmakers have become vertically integrated concerns (either through the investment in new technology or through acquisition) that Jaeger-LeCoultre has concentrated on its own watchmaking to a greater extent. Not since the 1920's and 1930's has Jaeger been so innovative and productive on their own watches as in the last two decades. The results are all too evident: victories at the only timing chronometry competition and other watch award events, one of the first to develop multi-axis tourbillons, and new innovations and acoustic quality in repeater watches.

Up until 1937 the watch firm was simply LeCoultre. Helmed by David LeCoultre (the third generation to take over the firm), the watch brand developed three product lines in the 1920's and 1930's that still exist today. In the middle of it all, David LeCoultre and Edmond Jaeger formed a partnership and the watchmaker: It was a challenge from Paris-based watchmaker, Edmond Jaeger to Swiss manufacturers to develop and produce the ultra-thin movements that he had invented. Jacques-David LeCoultre, who was responsible for production at LeCoultre & Cie., accepted the challenge, giving rise to a collection of ultra-thin pocket watches, including the thinnest in the world in 1907, equipped with the LeCoultre Calibre 145 mechanism?. The same year, French jeweller Cartier, one of Jaeger's clients, signed a contract with the Parisian watchmaker under which all Jaeger movements for a period of fifteen years would be exclusive to Cartier. The movements were produced by LeCoultre. The collaboration between Jaeger and LeCoultre led to the company being officially renamed Jaeger-LeCoultre in 1937.

A DECADE OF HOROLOGICAL PROWESS
(1926 – 1936)

The mark of a watchmaker in the 1920's was the ability to reduce the size of the movement, yet retain the timekeeping properties. The thinnest, smallest movement was the mark of the premier watchmaker. To that end, LeCoultre, as it was at that time, had not only notched up the thinnest movement on record, but was after the smallest.

The first step in 1926 was the Duometre movement. A simple idea, but one that allowed the size of the movement to be significantly reduced: take the thinnest movement, cut it in half, and put one part on top of the other! Seems self-evident now, but at the time, it allowed the movement size to be significantly reduced. The LeCoultre movement: 402 was the result. Over the next three years LeCoultre reduced the size of the movement to the smallest in the world at the time, and still the smallest today. The 101 remains the smallest and one of the most technically difficult watch movements to manufacture. Even after the passage of time, only approximately fifty 101 movements are manufactured in a year. The far eastern markets have become areas of high demand for the smallest of mechanical watches.

As LeCoultre's technical reputation for movement manufacture was being made, David LeCoultre was approached by Cesar de Trey to produce movements for a new watch: Reverso. By the time Cesar de Trey had acted upon the complaints of a British officer who had seen another watch die in the heat of battle on the polo field, LeCoultre had been manufacturing movements for the Parisian Edmond Jaeger, and the Parisian jeweller Cartier. Hence, perhaps unsurprisingly, when the design work was required for the new watch, it was given over to the Parisian engineer Alfred Chauvot, who in March 4, 1931, lodged a patent for a watch "..capable of revolving and sliding into its case". In November 1931, after having secured the rights to the Reverso from Alfred Chauvot, together with Jacques-David LeCoultre, César de Trey founded a company called Spécialités Horlogères. Hence, the first Reverso's were just that: Reverso. By 1937, with the change of name for the LeCoultre firm to Jaeger-LeCoultre, and the incorporation of the Reverso into the range of watches into the renamed firm, the Jaeger-LeCoultre Reverso really was Parisian, as much as it was Swiss.

The Reverso case is a classic of art deco design. Reverso's continue to this day as Jaeger-LeCoultre's flagship model; its timeless proportions (it is said that the dimensions of the case follow the divine ratio: phi) are as popular as they ever were. The range has varied from the classic size up to the new large bespoke sizes for such watches as the Tryptich and the Gyrotourbillon 2. All case sizes still have the same ratio of dimensions. Vintage Reverso's have become sought after not only for the vintage element, but for the story behind the watch itself. Because of the revolving case the reverse side to the case would be engraved or enameled. The Reverso was the watch of nobles and royalty where the family crest could be emblazoned on the reverse side of the watch. In one instance the watch was ordered for the future King Edward VIII, only to see the future monarch resign before he could be crowned.

The final model introduced in the 1930's was the ATMOS clock. The only watch or clock that has seen continuous production at Jaeger-LeCoultre since the acquisition of the patent by David LeCoultre in 1937. The invention and patenting of the ATMOS clock was undertaken by a young engineer from Neuchatel: Jean-Leon

Jaeger-LeCoultre AMVOX 7, collaboration with Aston Martin 2013
Photo: Andrew Hildreth

Bottom: Jaeger-LeCoultre Rose Gold Reverso Minute Repeater, with separate movement
and originalconcept pocket watch, set on patent document
Photos: Andrew Hildreth

Top: Jaeger-LeCoultre - the evolution of the smallest movement in the World ending with the JLC 101 on far right.
Bottom: Jaeger-LeCoultre Reverso with JLC 101 movement
Photos: Andrew Hildreth

Reutter. Although he did not formally study horology (he studied engineering), Reutter was nonetheless convinced that he could design and build a clock that would run on atmospheric fluctuations. The first prototype was developed in 1927. After developing the ATMOS prototype, Reutter joined the Compagnie Generale de Radiologie at Courbevoie (Ets. Gaiffe, Gallot et Pilon) as a radiology engineer. Despite being in full-time employment, and in a demanding area of science and engineering, by 1928 Reutter filed his patent on ATMOS I that was based on ammoniac and mercury. It is perhaps difficult to believe now, but no company in the Swiss (or American for that matter) watchmaking industry wanted to produce the clock. Up until 1937 the first ATMOS clocks were produced by a nuclear industry company!

While the nuclear engineering company put up the capital to produce the ATMOS clocks, it still required the actual clock mechanism from a specialist manufacturer. Initially this was subcontracted to a firm in Cluses in France. However, the initial mechanism was not of sufficient quality and a large number of clocks supplied were returned. The main problems were stoppages, the need for adjustment, and the fragility of the motor (especially in transit). Compagnie Generale came into contact with LeCoultre through Trevars Sales Company: the distributor of watches and clocks for Movado, LeCoultre, and Compagnie Generale ATMOS in the UK. By late 1932 LeCoultre were working on a movement for the clock. By 1935 Compagnie Generale had agreed to transfer its contracts with Reutter, plus the remaining stock of ATMOS clocks, to Edmund Jaeger Specialites Horlogeres SA (the distributor of Jaeger-LeCoultre products). In early 1936, LeCoultre was working on a simpler and more robust motor as the Jaeger-LeCoultre SA sales company was being formed. In two years, LeCoultre had a simplified ATMOS clock that would prove to be the working form for all variants of the ATMOS clock to follow.

ATMOS clocks continue to be sought after and a timepiece of reference for most collectors. It is the clock of Royalty, Presidents, Prime Ministers, and Popes. Today, demand for ATMOS clocks continues to grow and the market for secondhand ATMOS clocks has pushed auction prices higher. New variants of the clock that have seen modern designers collaborate with Jaeger-LeCoultre have breathed new life into the ATMOS line. The more notable of whom was Marc Newson. Newson, a life long fan of the ATMOS clocks, described his fascination with the ATMOS as a machine where you could observe the mechanism work; an analog experience in a digital age (where the time is simply recorded in digits on your phone, or on your computer screen).

RE-ASCENDENCY TO THE ZENITH (1991 – PRESENT)

The intervening years were not without memorable watches. The Memorvox and the Geophysic watches were very successful, and the re-issue of the watches in more modern form has increased auction prices for the vintage variant, but by the late 1980's Jaeger-LeCoultre existed almost only in name. The manufacturing element at Jaeger was reduced to producing base ebauche and cases, plus quartz watches.

In 1990 Jaeger-LeCoultre was bound together with IWC and Lange & Sohne in Les Manufactures Horologes (LMH) by Gunter Blumlein. With the takeover the fortunes of Jaeger-LeCoultre changed and have not looked back. In terms of watches, it was the Reverso model that led Jaeger-LeCoultre out of the dark ages of the quartz crisis. A series of six rose gold Reverso's that each contained a

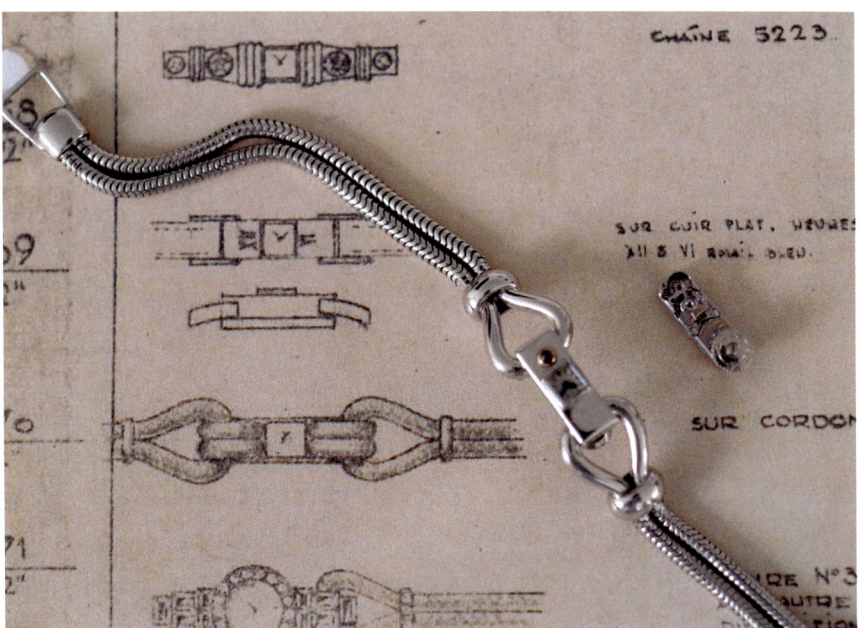

Jaeger-LeCoultre movement JLC 101 - smallest mechanical movement in the world,
and one example of it's jewellery timepieces.
Photo: Andrew Hildreth

complication were implemented during the 1990's decade. The reasons were two fold. The first was that the Reverso was the most recognizable watch that Jaeger-LeCoultre produced and that one form of promotion could cover all six models. The second was that nearly all the knowledge of how to build complications had been lost from the manufacture; it was a case of rebuilding both the knowledge base and the skilled watchmakers and designers to complete the watches. At the time, the marketing budget was limited, and the watches remained relatively hidden from the general watch buying public. Each watch came in a limited edition of 500 and today represent some of the better value for money haute horologerie on the market.

During the past decade Jaeger-LeCoultre has gone from strength to strength in terms of the variety and complexity of the watches produced. In particular, the Hybris Mechanica series has produced a number of tour de force complications involving multi-axis tourbillons, grand sonnerie repeating watches, and other innovations such as adjustable (to the nearest second) tourbillon watches and escapements that do not require lubrication.

The new watchmaking ethos and standard at Jaeger-LeCoultre has brought a number of watch awards with it. Not least among the prizes won was the first and second places at the newly instigated MIH Chronometry Competition in 2009; the regular single plane tourbillon outperforming (by a single point) the multi-axis tourbillon over the course of the competition. Other awards for design and watchmaking prowess have also been won. The increased complexity and finish on Jaeger-LeCoultre watches have likewise seen an increase in price to match. The price has stood up well in the auction market and some of the more recent limited editions will become tomorrow's classics for the Manufacture.

Numeral a re-drawing from an an Audemars Piguet Jules Audemars Chronograph

OBSERVATORY COMPETITIONS
PUBLISHER'S INTRODUCTION

Everyone likes competition, and nobody more than the mega companies of the luxury watch industry. 'One-upmanship' and 'betterings' of competitor's watches or their ability to keep time has always been a common theme amongst collectors trying to exemplify their latest purchases. Watchmakers alike are always trying to accomplish more than their peers or predecessors.

However, this is one area of both extreme intrigue and simultaneous fear for many watch manufacturing companies.

There have been a number of competitions over history in which watch brands can enter their highest complication pieces to determine who's is actually the best time keeper. The introduction of the tourbillon for example meant lesser movements did not stand much of a chance against the gravity defying balance wheel, and it is said that Seiko were even cast out of the competitions some years ago due to their springdrive and kinetic watches being too accurate! Greubel Forsey have devoted themselves to manufacturing the best tourbillon time keepers available, and they have successfully done so more than once, which is a phenomenal achievement for such a young brand.

Andrew Hildreth draws on his knowledge of the competitions, to describe what it takes to win them...

RACING THE HEAVENS!

OBSERVATORY COMPETITIONS AND THEIR IMPORTANCE IN WATCHMAKING

Andrew Hildreth

These days, something of an anachronistic event, the Chronometry Competition harks back a half-century or more, when watches were racing machines in an endurance duel against the heavens. The earth's rotation on its celestial path was the only known immovable timing device that kept time to the minute and second. Observatory timing contests were the horology equivalents of Grand Prix auto racing and the major watch firms of the day spent considerable resources on developing a winning watch. In 2009 the Observatory competitions were revived under the guise of the Horological Museum of Le Locle as the International Chronometry Contest.

Watches that won the Observatory competitions of the past were considered superlative timekeepers. Certainly many a reputation of current watch firms are built on their success during the Observatory competition years. Such was the need for extensive and independent testing that Observatory style competitions have been revived. However, without more support from the established brands, who used to use such tests to tout their prowess in watchmaking, the more recent incarnation of the Observatory competitions is unlikely to survive.

RACING THE HEAVENS IN THE PAST!

Observatory competitions, before the quartz crisis, had been the endurance car-racing equivalent for the watch industry. An often drawn analogy with the automotive world would be to think of the Observatory tests as being akin to the Le Mans 24 Hours. Only the difference here is that you cannot work on the watch during the racing. You can only pre-test as much as possible, but as the Observatory tests are being conducted, you can only hope that the watch both survives, and does not drop too many points. The observatories were the keepers of the time of day. They knew when the sun would rise and the heavens would disappear and then re-appear. At a certain longitude and latitude, given the earth's distance and rotational speed, sunrise, sunset, the pattern of the heavens would be computable to an exact hour, minute, and second.

Movement of the Patek Philippe 3834T
Photo: Andrew Hildreth

Patek Philippe 3834T, stunningly simple dial
Photos: Andrew Hildreth

Rolex ref. 6210 (1950s)
Photo: James Dowling

Ulysse Nardin Marine Chronometer
Photo: Ulysse Nardin

The idea for Observatory timing contests was initially instigated through a competition held at the observatory at Greenwich, London, England, in 1766. The reasons were fairly straightforward: if you had an accurate chronometer you could navigate across the world with greater precision. The determination of longitude (and where you were on the planet) required exact timing. Both the Royal Navy in England and the Navy in France offered substantial cash prizes to the timing competitions to encourage the development of marine chronometers and to find and acquire the most accurate versions on the market! The first chronometer competitions began in Geneva around 1790, but it was not until about 80 years later (in 1873) that the annual timing competitions were instigated for pocket chronometers. The international acceptance of the competitions was seen with the annual competitions being held at the Kew Observatory from 1884, and then subsequently in the following years at Besançon, Neuchâtel, Hamburg and Washington.

In all instances a points system was adopted, computed via a weighted sum, although unfortunately there was no standardized system between the observatories. Unlike current timing tests organised by Horological Museum of Le Locle and COSC (Contrôle Officiel Suisse des Chronomètres), in cooperation with the Swiss Society of Chronometry, the Observatory of Besançon, and the Haute-Ecole ARC Ingénierie, the past timing competitions would last for anywhere between 30 and 50 days. Points were deducted according to a weighted sum that was based on a variety of factors such heat, position, and shocks. Because of the differences between competitions, and the weighting and inclusion of factors affecting the final score (deduction), any comparison between Observatory competitions is problematic.

Considerable resources were expended by watch firms from the 1920's until the 1960's (both in Switzerland and in other countries where mechanical watches were made) to produce a mechanism, or more precisely an escapement, that would improve the chronometric performance of the watch throughout the five measuring positions (dial up, dial down, crown up, crown down and diagonally 45 degrees) and with varying temperature. Likewise after the event, favourable results in the competition would be publicized.

The masters of this were Rolex who would submit large numbers of movements for both the competitions and tests. The most stringent tests were from the Kew Observatory and watches with an 'A' grade were known to have passed at the highest score. In 1954 Rolex cased 24 movements that had obtained the Kew 'A' certificate and sold them as Ref 6210 (a simple gold case time only dialed watch). While the Rolex advertisements at the time claimed they were not special movements, infact, the movements were just that! In terms of details the escapement was free-sprung, with a Breguet overcoil, a Guillaume balance wheel, a very finely elaborated and finished pallet fork (to reduce weight as much as possible) and a hand made and very fine balance staff with very small pivots, to minimize friction as much as possible. They were the finest movements Rolex could, and arguably have, produced. Needless to say that with only 24 watches in existence the chances that they ever appear at auction is small to negligible. Generally, the Rolex ref. 6210 'Kew A' transfers between collectors for undisclosed prices.

Other firms that were 'regulars' at the Observatory Competitions were Patek Philippe, Omega, Ulysse Nardin, Longines, and Zenith. Of the approximately 4000 movements that received certificates from 1941 to 1967 at the two Swiss observatories (Geneva and Neuchatel), extremely few were cased and sold to the public. For example, Patek Philippe achieved 480 certificates, but only up to a maximum of 15 were ever cased and sold by the firm. Of the 15, 5 were the notable Patek reference 3834T, which was the highest scoring caliber at the Geneva Observatory. Once again, if ever the Patek Observatory chronometers come up for sale the price over the usual collectors' Patek price can be multiplied substantially (often running to 10 times the usual achieved price).

RESUMING THE CELESTIAL RACE!

Recently, the idea of Observatory competitions has been revived and held under the title of the Horological Museum of Le Locle International Chronometry Contest. Added into the mix of requirements in more recent Chronometry competitions are the anti-magnetic and shock tests that previously had not been part of the Observatory tests, but now had to be accommodated in regulating a watch for the Horological Museum of LeLocle Chronometry Competition. The degree of difficulty in the tests gives weight to different aspects of watches performance under different conditions. First, there is the variation in location. The first test is held at Besancon, the second at Bienne (COSC), the watches are then delivered to an engineering school for the shock and magnetism tests, and given they are still running, they are delivered back to Bienne (COSC) for a final third set of (15 day) timing tests. The complete set of timing tests are in the five positions for the watch on the wrist over a total of 45 days.

The nature of the tests are such that a variation of +/- 2 seconds a day would be sufficient to see the watch finish so far down the list that it would never win. Alternatively, another way of gauging just how accurate the watches need to be, a single variation of 5 seconds a day (at any point over the course of the tests) would be sufficient to knock the score down to an unrecoverable position. Out of 1000 points that you start with, it is the watch that loses the least points, that is the winner. The time variation of +/- 2 seconds a day (throughout the course of the tests) would be sufficient to see the watch lose approximately 700 points and be placed far down the list. The winning score in 2009 for the Jaeger-LeCoultre 978 Master Tourbillon was 909 points. The winning score for the Greubel Forsey Double Tourbillon Technique in 2011 was 915. What does that translate to in the variation in seconds (on average) across the 45 days of the testing? It translates into a variation of +/- 0.3 to +/- 0.8 seconds a day. To put that number in perspective, it is the kind of variation quoted in the more accurate of the quartz chronometers when worn normally on the wrist (with no abnormal or adverse shocks or other treatments). An astounding degree of accuracy!

It is difficult to compare timing competition tests over time, however, from the formulas that Greubel Forsey found in the archives. If the timing data is entered and a score computed, the Double Tourbillon Technique would out score all! It is only a hypothetical, as there is always a degree of uncertainty in competition, but the results are illustrative of how escapement design and time keeping have moved forward.

Technology may have caught up with the tourbillon. The need for precision in the manufactured parts, that makes the tourbillon a more precise chronometric device, has only become possible in recent years through dedicated research by a number of firms. Although in the earlier Observatory competitions, the regular balance wheel would stand the same chance as the tourbillon; recent results suggest that the tourbillon now stands out as a more precise escapement. I have heard this, not just from Robert Greubel and Stephen Forsey, but other watchmakers at other firms with complex tourbillon escapement designs. Correctly adjusted, the multi-axis tourbillon is the superior escapement.

As the latest MIH Chronometry Competition continues to roll around each year, there is still resistance from the watch industry. Where are some of the 'big guns' of the haute horologerie world who make claims and yet are unwilling to enter an independent competition, where all rules are known, and where all the watches are on an equal footing? For all their concentration on decoration and technique, Greubel Forsey watches are also shown, against all the other watches entered, to be the reigning champions. Past glories are just that: yesterday's news.

Haute horologerie should be about designing, inventing, and manufacturing watches that improve chronometric performance: not just on a one-off basis as the Observatory competition pieces once were, but in the general production of watches that are sold to collectors. In preparing for the 2009 competition, Jaeger-LeCoultre learned in testing that the balance wheel in their watches had to be altered. This alteration then became part of their regular production. There was learning that was translated into regular production watches that improve chronometric performance. Watches do not have to be dull in design, the Greubel Forsey Double Tourbillon Technique is arguably one of the most impressive watch designs of the last decade, and yet for all the innovative design, this is still a watch that tells the time accurately. There is still innovation, but there is improved time keeping. Surely this must be the best of all worlds.

Numeral a re-drawing from a Cartier Ballon Bleu Extra Flat

INDUSTRY PROFILES
PUBLISHER'S INTRODUCTION

During my time in the watch industry I have been fortunate to meet some exceptionally inspiring experts with interesting minds. Whether the chairman of a retail group, heavyweight private dealer, collector or visionary behind a brand, there is one element gluing everyone together – passion for watches. These passions appear in different shapes and sizes, with views one might not expect.

This is a chapter designed for our readers to really 'meet the man'. This chapter introduces some of these individuals to our readers, giving some conversational introduction to the people behind the industry, an industry we find so enjoyable; individuals who support the educational and conversational style of Twelve, and who we are proud to say are our friends.

In this issue we speak to:

Charlie Pragnell
of George Pragnell Fine Jewellery

Giles English
of Bremont Choronometers

Jorn Werdelin and Morten Linde
of Linde Werdelin

David Coleridge
of The Watch Gallery

CHARLIE PRAGNELL

Interview with Charlie Pragnell by Jacob Tomkins

George Pragnell Ltd, in Stratford-upon-Avon. The Pragnells are known to have been the best jewellers outside London for three generations, and Charlie has now taken over the business. It is 10am and I sit with Charlie in the empty dining room of a traditional private members club in Mayfair. The atmosphere is friendly and jovial, and Charlie is a faultless host. His energy andenthusiasm for the business come through his every word.

Q. How did the Pragnells business start?

"Well..."[he starts, suggesting that the story is reassuringly neither short or simple]

"George Pragnell is a culmination of several different businesses from the past. Pragnells itself was always jewellery and antique silver. Watches have become more significant since the mid 80s when Americans visiting the UK started buying gold Rolex watches. In the 70s it was normal for people in Switzerland to own multiple watches. Now the UK is only really how Switzerland was 30-40 years ago. The idea of watches being like a piece of jewellery, and that you'd own more than one, has expanded outwards from Switzerland, across the world.

But in terms of understanding the family business, for example; we own a business that is 100 years this year called Tarratt (George Tarratt was a great expert in silver from Leicestershire). A lot of our silver knowledge comes from there, and where we still base workshops. Before moving to Stratford upon Avon in 1954, my Grandparents ran Biggs of Maidenhead – jeweller to Queen Mary. We owned Philip Antrobus, supplier of the Queen's engagement ring, which was the oldest shop on Old Bond Street – rich in antique jewellery history.

A year after I was married I realised my wife had relatives from the Garrard family. A coincidence that somehow felt inevitable!
The point is; we have gleaned knowledge from our experiences with a lot of different businesses, individuals and apprenticeships over the time in watches,

Patek Philippe 5025G
Photos: Watchclub/Michal Solarsk

jewellery and silver. We have also worked in clocks, which is not irrelevant to the world of watches. So the business today is an amalgamation of all these parts."

Q. How would you compare the customers on the jewellery side of the business to the watch side?

"Fine jewellery is worn by women, mechanical watches are worn by men and women - generally speaking - but otherwise it's impossible to compare them. There are certain patterns to buying, in terms of everyday watches and jewellery and more formal watches and jewellery. Special moments traditionally call for jewellery, but this is becoming the case with watches now.

The most important thing when buying the watch is that you love it – that it suits what you're wearing, what you're doing and that it suits your lifestyle. When a watch is more expensive people are more concerned with residual value. Holding value is important to buyers, but they know it's at least 5-10 years before most actually appreciate."

Q. As an authorized retailer, have you noticed a downturn in sales since the internet has become a prominent buying tool and you can get 'second hand deals' easily online?

"We also sell 'second hand' watches so we understand both markets.

New watches contain the most up to date movement technology and the best new materials in a developing market. Tastes and styles evolve and within the iconic watch houses the classics are constantly refined and improved.

People may choose to buy second hand goods instead of new, the world over. You can't compare one customer to another, but the internet has contributed to growth in our industry rather than a lull. All the brands we carry have had more exposure from the internet, so quite simply more people buy new and 'second hand' watches.

Q. What was your first watch?

" A 1960s IWC Portofino Yellow Gold, inherited from my mother's father when I was 18yrs old. I wore it on our wedding day – I was particularly fond of my mother's father, who actually was from a 6th generation jewellery manufacturing business – another member of the family in the trade!"

Q. Were you always going to be involved in the family business, and when did you decide to be?

"Well....it's difficult not to be! When you're growing up with it going on all around you. I wasn't necessarily conscious of it all going on when I was very young, and I remember seeing various objects and processes in and out of the business, and perhaps that affected my interests, but when I left university I went to see what the City was all about, and looked at a variety of sectors for a year or two.

I didn't feel particularly passionate or compelled by anything I found, and having run a business at university I knew I wanted to run my own again. It was a matter of what sort. I was fortunate enough to find a passion in gemstones initially. I realised I should probably have a chat about how that might work! I then did my apprenticeships in various parts of the world and came back, and now I'm running it."

Q. Your apprenticeship was in antique jewellery and rare gemstones?

"Yes - the mainstays of our business."

Q. Would you say your loose gemstone customers are buying as investments, similar to watch clients, in that they are considered a convenient transportable asset?

"Well, yes, but customers would mount the stone in jewellery so that you could wear it. The point and similarity here [between gemstones and watches] is that the rarer and more attractive the article the more likely it is to become a more desirable object in the future. So our loose stone customers will mount them in jewellery to make them so. That's the way the gemstone and watch world are similar in one way – the bigger it is, the better it is, the rarer it is, the more wearable it is; the more likely it is to appreciate over time. That's true."

Q. Five watches you've bought for yourself, or would buy, that you feel will increase in value, but also that you love.

"I don't buy watches based on the fact that they will appreciate in value – I'm in the business, so if I think something will increase in value I look after the collectors. Often watches are in limited production and highly valuable, and my job is to look after the collectors...
I buy a watch if there is a particular occasion that I wish to mark – it's a personal marking of a moment – that's how I look at it.
But, if I got into speculation or collecting iconic watches, there are so many watches that I'd want to buy!

So, hypothetically speaking:"

1. Patek Nautilus Chronograph in Rose Gold on a Bracelet –
"Fantastic watch. So cool. We're going from a white metal decade-or-two into a gold metal decade in terms of what people will be wearing, in my opinion."

2. Patek Philippe 5205r, open lugs, black dial.
"To me, it's just a very stylish, gentlemen's dress watch with a useful annual calendar complication."

3. Cartier Tank MC in Rose Gold
"a very smart classic with a good automatic movement."

Q. You really think we're going into Rose gold era?!

"Oh yeah, no doubt, it already is!"

4. Rolex Explorer I Steel
"such an understated, perfectly proportioned sports watch. And it's as bullet proof as you're going to get."

5. "The last I'd have to buy for my wife, or I'd be in trouble! Which would be Patek Philippe 7200R, a beautifully elegant ladies wristwatch."

Q. Any closing points for collectors?

"A. Lange Sohne – the quality of Lange is absolutely superb, and the fact they come from a different place, both geographically and in their approach, all makes them very appealing and popular among collectors. Go and see their 1815 Rattrapante Perpetual Calendar chronograph in rose gold, then inspect the pinnacle of watchmaking that is the Patek Philippe 5208P, ...and then retire."

GILES ENGLISH

Interview with Giles English by Jacob Tomkins

Giles English is a co-founder of Bremont Watches, along with his brother Nick. Having launched their own London boutique in 2012 Giles has realised a long-term dream to build a British horological brand from scratch, and they've done so in true British style. Sober, jolly, excitable and innovative - Giles and I sit and reminisce about their early pieces, and play with the new ones, as we discuss his love for the industry, the products and his business.

Q. What is the story of the start of the Bremont brand?

GE - It all started off with our father, an amazing engineer, who had a passion for planes, clocks, watches and all things mechanical., As children we spent our days in the workshop and sharing our passions with him. In 1995 he had a plane crash with my brother, he sadly died and Nick broke over 30 bones. This accident was the catalyst/turning point in life for us to do something we loved and we decided to build a watch company. I had trained as an engineer and we were running a small engineering business restoring historical machines. We went to Switzerland and spent 5 yrs working hard before we were ready to launch our first watch.

Q. Why watches, e.g. not planes or motorbikes?

GE - Our aim was to bring watch making back home to the UK and we felt there was opportunity in what we wanted to offer in the mechanical watch market.

Q. What was the original vision for the products?

GE - To create a classical styled watch that you could wear in the boardroom or up Mount Everest

Omega Speedmaster Professional Moonwatch
Photo: Watchclub

Q. Biggest challenges in manufacturing watches?

> GE - Every thing to do with manufacturing watches is a challenge and as you grow these challenges increase. Naturally for us doing it in the UK there is a huge challenge of finding the skills required for watch making.

Q. What was your first mechanical watch?

> GE - A 50's Omega given to me by my grandfather, which I still have.

Q. How do/did you go about collecting?

> GE - For us it was vintage watch collecting 20 years ago when the market was very different and it was mostly old vintage aviation watches. You could pick them up for very little money then.

Q. Watches as investments…what is your opinion on this subject?

> GE - Ultimately buy for the love of the watch but I do believe the market is still growing considerably and the cost of manufacturing watches is not coming down. I have seen some considerably good investments in watches and some very bad ones. I am happy to say that our Limited Edition watches have been rather impressive.

Q. Name 3-5 watches that you would buy today for yourself if you had the chance… Your favourite pieces.

> GE - I would naturally go for vintage watches and some of the classics are;
> 1. Omega Speedmaster
> 2. 801 Navitimer Breitling
> 3. Smiths W10 Pilot watch
> 4. any George Daniels Watch

Q. Best experience of working in the industry? And/or biggest challenges faced in the industry?

> GE- This is a wonderful industry to be in and we have really been helped out by manufactures, other watch companies, retailers and press. One of my greatest first highs was when we saw our watches for the first time which was in Watch Gallery - Fulham Road, and seeing our first sales go through. The biggest challenge we face is introducing new watch makers and skilled craftsman into the industry as the market grows.

DAVID COLERIDGE
THE WATCH GALLERY CHAIRMAN

Interview with David Coleridge by Jacob Tomkins

I sit with David in his glass office where we chat openly and frankly about the market, his experiences, and his business. There is an air of absolute efficiency in his work environment, supported by the wonderful yet empirical charts he has on nearly everything in the industry, from the flow and stretch of Rolex sales in the UK, to maps and plans of his business models... a truly enjoyable spirit and clearly the main stimulant behind the success of his company.

Q. Are you a man of watch passion??

I didn't start out as a watch man! But they grow on you...

As a buyer one becomes more dispassionate in business. You'll go bankrupt quickly if not...but of course I have a soft spot for watches now. I don't even make watch buying decisions for my business any more. I have two buyers whose jobs are in many ways the dream job of a collector. They make all the buying decisions for us.

At SIHH this year we'll spend large sums on stock orders, and I wont choose a single watch! We wouldn't buy a brand unless I've agreed to buy it of course... But one has to be dispassionate in our position. Every year we reduce our offering by a few brands – some years half a dozen.

The only watch I tried on in my latest trip to Geneva was the Tudor Titanium Pelagos, with the new clasp mechanism. I would buy this over a Rolex Submariner or a GMT Master II – I loved it. This desire must come from a rooted passion.

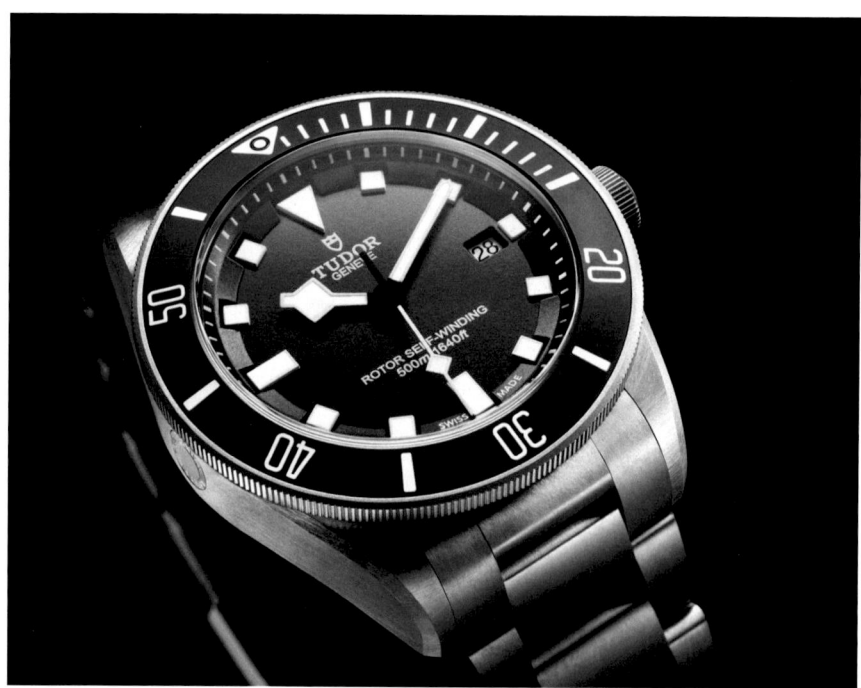

Tudor Pelagos
Photo: Tudor

Tudor Pelagos
Photo: Tudor

Q. 'How did you get into the business?'

By mistake!...
I joined Dunhill in 1983, thinking I was joining a tobacco company, as Print Buyer. I was very fortunate - two or three of the marketing people left in the following months so I was quickly promoted, and then invited to work in Japan. So I went for seven years. 1986-1992. Spent wonderful time there during the 'bubble economy', with gold leaf on your sushi and vast business success happening. Something was wrong if you didn't have 50% annual growth at that time.

Dunhill was part of Dunhill Holdings, which over the next few years morphed into Vendome, which was known for the Cartier group. Vendome then morphed into Richemont Intl.
I came back to the UK and for five years as Managing Director of Hackett (which was a complete anomaly for the Richemont Group. A soft clothing brand! Richemont can't do soft!) That was the only time I spent in the UK with the company. I then went to Hong Kong, then back to Japan, then to Russia...

None of my work was specialist watches, but it was all luxury goods, and the group is dominated by Cartier, (making up 75% of Richemont total revenue). I worked with A.Lange Sohne, Jaeger-LeCoultre, IWC, Mont Blanc, Panerai, Dunhill – all 11 companies in the region. My job was to tie them all together under the new group.

I spent my final 4 years at Richemont reporting to the brilliant man that is Alain Perri - the creator of the modern Cartier. The job was gravitating back to Geneva and, frankly at this stage, I wanted to stay in the UK. So after 21 years, call it a mid-life crisis if you will (!), I decided I wanted to do it myself. So, I found that a lot of my friends who were in banking were in fact in private equity, so advice was plentiful. Through friends of friends I came across Huntsman, the Saville Row tailor and became an investor in that. I ran it part time, one day a week. Through more friends of friends I met the prolific watch and jewellery retailer David Morris, who wanted advice about going to Russia, which I gladly gave. As I was walking out the door he asked "So, what are you doing now?".

"I'm trying to buy a business", I said.

His response was immediate – "OH! Do you want to buy mine?! – I've got a watch business"

It was a small watch business- four concessions in Selfridge, which I bought in 2006, and that is where DM London started.
The luxury business which we have now under The Watch Gallery umbrella has stores in Westfield, in Chelsea and a Rolex boutique in One Hyde Park. Then we also have the concessions floor in Selfridges, and the Watch Gallery online. In six years we've grown four times bigger. It's gone pretty well.

Q. So what was the business vision when you bought it?'

> Completely different! The business plan I gave to my co-investors in 2006 concentrated on the lower, designer end of the market, and totally failed to even mention the existence of the internet. It mainly involved rolling out designer concessions in department stores.
>
> Our current claim to success; after Aurum Group (Watches Of Switzerland / Mappin and Webb) we're the next biggest retailer of Rolex in the country, and we only have three doors. Aurum have 44. Our Rolex boutique in Knightsbridge is a big notch on the belt for us. Luckily the brands are pretty receptive when a new, fast growth focused, entrepreneurial retailer come around like us.

Q. How do you use the Internet, and how do you see it's role in the business and your industry?

> UK, In December 2013, 20% of all retail sales were online. We are investing heavily in the internet and continually learning, and although there is no money to be made yet for us, everyone is still heavily investing. We like to think we know more about the Internet than any other UK watch retail business.
>
> An online shop is every bit as expensive as opening a shop on the highstreet. You have to spend a great deal on marketing to get the website visible whereas on the high street you are immediately visible with the right location.
>
> Google owns the high street – Google was not built to give you unbiased and efficient search, Google was invested to make money, and it is the most amazing money machine. We love google and spend large sums on their advertising platforms.
>
> We have a team of about 35people just working on the websites. The interenet is big cost and focus, and holds a lucrative future for our industry. We are at the stage now that 32% of the watches on thewatchgallery.com are transactable… it was zero when we started.
>
> Customer desire in terms of purchasing process has dictated our online customer proposition. There are many watches being transacted online through the website. However, most customers still like to pick up the phone to have a good old telephone conversation. The development of the internet has been purely and simply down the request of the customer and the information they want to help them make their decision more easily.

Q. What is the vision of the business?

The vision takes us to being the vest retailer of watches in the UK. That's the ambition. We can't be the biggest – Aurum have 180 stores on the high street. But if we are the retailer of choice for the brands, then we will be the retailer of the choice of the consumers as well.

Our tunnel vision is that watchgallery.co.uk is the best watch retailing website in the UK – the UK is so far ahead of the rest of world online that if we are the best in the UK, theoretically we will be the best in the world.

An example we're proud of is that we are selling ten times more Tag Heuer watches on our website than TagHeueur.com

Tank Louis Cartier XL slimline Rose Gold
Photo: Cartier

Q. What was your first mechanical watch:

My first real watch was the Dunhill Automatic Full Calendar Automatic Moon Phase – I worked for Dunhill so I had to wear it, but it has a fantastic Zenith El RPimero movement.

Q. How do you choose what you buy for yourself?

I like alarm watches, because I like to use the functions. – I had a Dunhill Millennium (made in 1983/1984) which were hugely successful pieces but largely quartz. I probably have 30-40 watches covering 10-15 brands, but its all about function for me as a buying routine.

I do love my Hublot big bang yellow (number 5/10), mainly as it was a limited edition specially for us to celebrate the Selfridges 100th anniversary. A sweet memory. It was the first time a brand gave us an exclusive. Loving a watch is equally important, for whatever reason.

Q. What is your favourite watch in your collection?

My Steel on brown leather PAM098 - If I had to throw all my watches away, this is the one I'd keep. Bought it in 2002 the after we bought the business. I just love it.

Q. Watches as investments. Whats your opinion?

I think it's a tough way to make money. I would rarely buy a watch as an investment, because when I buy one I want to wear it, and if you wear a watch, it depreciates. The number one rule for buying is that you love it. As I say, for me watches are about function and I've never really looked at them as investments.
Some hold their residual value better than others quite effectively though– similar to vintage cars.

Truly, if you love the watch, as you would love the wine or vintage car, and you can make a bit of money – fantastic. The key is to first know what you're doing as a buyer.

Q. Three watches that you would buy today.

1. Tudor Pelagos Titanium – alternative or grade up from my holiday watch.
2. Panerai 18k Rose gold Radiomir PAM 0513
3. Something awful and bling I suppose! I love AP but I don't have the balls to wear it! It's the Tank Louis Cartier Extra Flat Rose Gold

MORTEN LINDE
AND
JORN WERDELIN

Interview by Jacob Tomkins

Morten Linde and Jorn Werdelin are the co-founders of Linde Werdelin – a brand that has recently become recognisable and extremely popular for its industrial and modern designs, and use of unusual materials. Their watches are designed and built around the modern, adventurous collector, with digital instruments especially made to fit the watches for diving and skiing activities. The two are Danish born childhood friends, with a classically dry Scandinavian air of quality and precision about them. Both with a long standing passion for watches and strong entrepreneurial spirits, they answer questions about how they feel about designing watches, working in the industry, their customers and the business in general.

Q. Morten - How did watch design start for you?

> (ML) I studied in the late 80s as a product designer in Denmark, but it was impossible to BE a product designer in Denmark at that time, so I began in furniture, working with shapes and materials for people's homes. I graduated in 1990 and worked for Daniel Levinson for two years, and in 1992 I opened my own design studio. I took some watch prototype designs to Basel the following year and it all started there...

Q. Why watches?

> (ML) I had been around watches since I was 16. My first watch was a Rolex, and I was fascinated with the mechanics, and in fact everything about them. From a design point of view - that they are so complicated; the way they fit the wrist; the tolerances and ergonomics, that they could last for 100 years. Something that lasts a long time is a great pleasure to design.

Q. Jorn - Where did your watch passion come from?

> (JW) Well...my very earliest memories include watches and jewellery since my family had been in the business for generations. I suppose it is almost part of my DNA!

Left: Jorn-Werdelin
Right: Morten Linde

Urwerk UR110-ST
Photo: Urwerk

Q. Why enter such a competitive and noisy sector with a new brand?

(ML) Jorn and I had similar situations in different industries – we both had great clients and good work, but after finishing work for clients and handing over our respective deliverables, there was no more involvement in the projects. We wanted more depth and more ownership in our work. Starting the brand was a big challenge but a necessary one. Our combined love and 'DNA' made watches an obvious choice.

Q. What was the original overall vision for Linde Werdelin?

(JW) The core idea has always been the same, coloured by our very personal vision: timepieces that can withstand sports such as skiing and diving, namely, and overall enhance the overall experience.
Striking a balance between aesthetics and functionality was also a key point. In our view, the best way of telling time is with an analog watch however, for sports, you need digital precision.
This is where our high performance skiing and diving instruments come into the picture, attaching seamlessly to the timepieces.

Q. Morten - What are the biggest challenges in running the brand, from a designers viewpoint?

(ML) The biggest challenge is the supply chain – fitting all the elements and materials together with the right timing and precision. But, as a designer, there is never a problem without a solution, and design is really all about solving problems. I try to turn the problem into a particularity of the design – for example, the need to attach a dive or ski instrument to the watch inspired the case designs.

Q. What is you favourite aspect of watch design?

(ML) Different artisans - without question. The ability to work with so many different skills and specialities, and the combination of my design and their skill is a relationship like no other. It gives me great pleasure to work alongside these traditions and methods...

Q. How do you both feel about watch collectors and enthusiasts as customers?

(JW) The reason we are where we are today is because we were embraced early on by watch collectors and the industry overall.
Since the beginning, we have endeavoured to keep an open dialogue with such customers, and have learned from them along the way. We consider our customers and enthusiasts to be part of the extended LW family.

Top: Urwerk UR110-ST (back)
Photo: Urwerk
Bottom: Jaeger-LeCoultre Reverso Rose Gold
Photo: Andrew Hildreth

Q. Jorn - What was your first mechanical watch?

(JW – straight to jump on this question) It was probably a Cartier Santos, which I bought as a teenager.

Q. Watches as investments – What is your opinion?

(JW) In my view, they are less of an investment and more something that is to be enjoyed. That is really true luxury.
On another note, because our watches are all limited editions, their inherent value is reinforced and quality is more consistent overtime.

Q. Three watches you would buy today / that you love for under £50k?

(JW) if I must!...
1. JLC Reverso Gran Sport in gold case
2. URWERK - 110
3. Richard Mille - RM011

GLOSSARY

Bracelet	Metal or hard material wrist strap.
Case	Main body housing movement.
Chronograph	Stop-watch complication.
Chronometry	Study of the measurement of time.
Co-Axial	Patented automatic movement by George Daniels (Chapter 10).
Complication	Additional mechanical feature of the movement beyond hours, minutes and seconds.
Crown	Main control knob for adjusting time and other functions.
Dial	Internal face holding timing markings.
Ebauche	Watch movement and parts in unassembled state.
Escapement	Movement part which controls and counts the timekeeping energy transfer.
GMT	Second time zone function.
Grand Complication	Movement with several complications.
Haute Horology/Horlogerie	Literally "High Horology" - used by brands to define themselves as high quality manufacture.
Horology	The study of watchmaking.
Main Spring	Spiral spring used as power source in mechanical watches
Mechanical	A watch with no electronic parts, either automatic or manual wind.
Minute Repeaters	Complication which signifies time through chiming.
Movement	The internal mechanism or mechanical engine.
Perpetual Calendars	Complications which track leap years and can quantify days of the month continually, without resetting.
Quartz Crisis	or "Quartz Revolution" Era of evolution of the electronic quartz watch that in turn challenged mechanical watchmaking, 1970s and early 1980s.
Sidereal Time	Astronomic timekeeping system. "Briefly, sidereal time is a "time scale that is based on the Earth's rate of rotation measured relative to the fixed stars. " *Wikipedia*
Tonneau	Case shape with broad, rounded edges.
Tourbillon	Highly accurate timekeeping movement part which greatly lessens the general effects of gravity on a mechanical escapement and mvoement.
Trebauchet	Part of movement which acts like a catapult.
Valjoux	Movement manufacturing company.

A SPECIAL THANK YOU TO:

Alastair Laidlaw, Andrew Hildreth, Ben Clymer, Ben Katzler, Charlie Pragnell, Dan Rolfe Johnson, Darius Delauney-Driquert, Diamantis Diamantidis, Dino Costas, Eliana Tomkins, Evan Zimmerman, Ghazi Daghistani, Giles English, Giovanna Del Sarto, Gus Oliver, James Dowling, James Gurney, Jamie Wood, Jonathan Scatchard, Jorn Werdelin, Joseph Mackenzie, Justin Jay Koullapis, Ken Kessler, Laurie Milne, Luke Button, Luke Waite, Marcus Watson, Max Busser, Meera Anand, Michal Solarski, Morten Linde, Ray Tomkins, Rob Hersov, Robert Wilson, Robert-Jan Broer, Sarah Hue-Williams, Scott Levy, Simon de Burton, Stephen J. Pulvirent, Thibaux Jouen…and anyone else who has supported us along the way.

175

ISBN 9780992837600

Clemens Fritsch
Thomas Ruzicka

Fluorescence Diagnosis
and Photodynamic Therapy
of Skin Diseases

Atlas and Handbook

SpringerWienNewYork

PD. Dr. Clemens Fritsch
Privatpraxis für Dermatologie, Allergologie and Venerologie,
Düsseldorf, Germany

Univ.-Prof. Dr. Dr. h.c. Thomas Ruzicka
Hautklinik, Universität Düsseldorf, Germany

This work is subject to copyright.
All rights are reserved, whether the whole or part of the material is concerned, specifically those of translation, reprinting, re-use of illustrations, broadcasting, reproduction by photocopying machines or similar means, and storage in data banks.

Product Liability: The publisher can give no guarantee for the information contained in this book. This also refers to that on drug usage and application thereof. In each individual case the respective user must check the accuracy of the information given by consulting other pharmaceutical literature. The use of registered names, trademarks, etc. in this publication does not imply, even in the absence of a specific statement, that such names are exempt from the relevant protective laws and regulations and therefore free for general use.

© 2003 Springer-Verlag/Wien
Printed in Slovenia

Typesetting and Printing: Gorenjski Tisk, 4000 Kranj, Slovenia

Printed on acid-free and chlorine-free bleached paper
SPIN: 10878201

With 266 coloured Figures

CIP-data applied for

ISBN 3-211-83827-9 Springer-Verlag Wien New York